# God's Promise *for* You

GREAT
COMMISSION
MEDIA

*"I know the plans that I have for you,"*
*declares the Lord.*

Jeremiah 29:11

# Dr. Charles F. Stanley

# God's Promise *for* You

*Discovering His will for your life*

Published in Atlanta, Georgia, by Great Commission Media, LLC.

All Scripture quotations, unless otherwise noted, are taken from the *NEW AMERICAN STANDARD BIBLE®*, Copyright © 1960, 1962, 1963, 1968, 1971, 1972, 1973, 1975, 1977, 1995 by The Lockman Foundation. Used by permission.

ISBN: 0-9770976-0-9

Requests for information should be addressed to:
Great Commission Media
P.O. Box 548
Lebanon GA 30146

To discover other Charles Stanley teaching resources,
visit www.charlesstanleyinstitute.com or www.intouch.org

# CONTENTS

# Does God Have A Plan for Me?

*D*"Does God have a purpose and a plan for my life? If so, can I know it?" Each time I hear these two questions, I answer the same way, Yes, He does. In fact, His personal promise to you is that He does have a purpose and a plan for your life (Jeremiah 29:11). While you may not know or understand all the twists and turns of life, you can be sure of one thing: the same God who breathed life into you, loves you enough to plan for your future. He has promised that if you will seek Him, you will find Him and you also will discover His will for your life.

Many people spend a lot of time thinking about how God's will is a mystery that cannot be unlocked. This simply is not true. We can know the plans He has for us. We may not know all the details because God keeps some aspects of His will to Himself, but we can know the right path to take in every situation.

Years ago, I wrote a small book entitled *Discovering God's Will*. In it, I included some of the questions people asked on a regular basis. Each one involved some aspect of God's will for their lives. At that time, most of the questions focused on potential marriage partners, raising children, and selecting the right vocation.

Today, however, many questions we face have changed. Following the world events of the past few years, the questions are much more intense and include ones such as the following:

- Yesterday, I received word that I was going to be laid off from my job. My wife is out of work also, and I don't know how we will pay our mortgage. Does God have a plan for us? I need to know because I feel so hopeless.
- I'm thirty-one years old and my doctor told me last week that I have cancer. I don't understand. I love God and have been living my life for Him. Why is He allowing this to happen? Does He have a purpose for my suffering?
- Last week, my doorbell rang and I opened the door to a sight that I feared would come. Two

army officers stood before me with the news my
son had been killed in battle. My grief is so great.
I don't understand God's will at all. My son was
so young. What is God doing? Is there a way that
He will use this for some purpose in the future?

- I never realized I could feel so lonely. However,
  after my husband left me last year, I have strug-
  gled with deep feelings of loneliness and even
  fear. Does God still have a plan for me? Will I
  ever feel happy and alive again?

- For several years, I used various drugs. Today,
  thanks to God's help and the support of my church
  family, I am drug free. However, now I feel so
  shameful. Can God still use me? Does He have a
  plan for my life? Is there hope for my future?

Without a doubt, today more and more people
are wondering if God is aware of their situation and
the problems they are facing. However, the deeper
question is, "Does He love me and have a purpose
for my life?"

Let me start this book with some very good
news. In spite of any difficulty or sin that you may
have faced, God still has a fantastic plan in mind for
your life. This is His personal promise for you. It is

His plan to give you hope and a future, and it is His goal to lead you through the difficult times as well as the good times so that you will fulfill His purpose in this life. In Proverbs, He says, when we turn to Him and place the focus of our hearts on Him, "He will make our paths straight" (Proverbs 3:5-6).

For someone reading these words, the idea of traveling a straight path is very encouraging, especially if you have spent years wandering in circles that include pathways that God never designed for you to travel. However, all of that is about to change as you discover His will for your life, which includes a plan that is tailored perfectly to suit you. Many people want to know, "How can I be sure that I am doing the right thing? Will God tell me?" The answer is yes!

He will never leave you groping for answers. You may have to spend some time seeking His face for answers to your prayers, but when you do, you will never be disappointed. He is the only One who knows the plans that He has for us and how they can be fulfilled. They are plans that contain renewed peace and joy.

It is my heart's prayer that everyone who reads

this book will allow God to demonstrate His infinite love and care for him or her in a fresh new way. Without a doubt, once you accept Christ as your Savior, the most important aspect of the Christian life is learning that He has a will and purpose not only for your eternal life but for every situation you face each day.

It all begins with faith in an all-powerful, loving Savior who has your very best in mind—always. Once you place your faith in Him, nothing can hold you back from gaining the peace and contentment that He has for you. My question to you is this: Are you ready to take the next first step to discovering exactly what God has planned for you? Don't miss another moment that could be spent in the blessing He promises each one of us.

Charles F. Stanley
Atlanta, Ga.

# CHAPTER ONE

# The Big Picture

"Does God have a plan for me?" the young man asked. His face was etched with worry and regret. He had come to know Christ as his Savior years before during a youth rally, but now, sitting in my office, he was not only on the verge of doubting his salvation but also God's love for him. He could not see past the sin that was in his life nor could he accept God's forgiveness, and this was choking the spiritual life out of him.

I reassured him that while there were consequences to sin, God still had a plan and a purpose for his life. He never gives up on us. Even though he had made mistakes and at one point ignored God's leading, the Lord loved Him and heard his prayers. God would not ignore him or push him aside.

## *A Future And A Hope*

"God loves you," I reassured him (John 3:16; Jeremiah 31:3). "He created you, and He is not about to give up on you—not now—not ever. You can depend on this." Instantly, silence filled the room. I could sense that God had broken through and for the first time in a very long time, this young man's mind and heart were tuned into the voice of God. Then I repeated a familiar verse to him—one that most of us have come to know by heart and that is Jeremiah 29:11. "'I know the plans that I have for you,' declares the Lord, 'plans for welfare and not for calamity to give you a future and a hope.'"

Leaning forward, I looked straight into my young friend's eyes and said, "You realize this is not Charles Stanley talking. This is God speaking to you. I don't have all the answers, but there is one thing that I do know and that is this: *God knows exactly where you are at this very minute, and He understands your every struggle (Psalm 46:1).* He is the one who has all the answers you need and each one is found within His Word. He may not like where your life is right now, but He is not going to abandon you (John 14:18). If you will trust Him, He will begin to work in your life. Then you will see His plan and will for your life unfold in a mighty way. This is His promise to each one of us."

My words were hitting their right mark because the young man relaxed and drew in a deep breath. "You mean there is hope for my life?"

"Absolutely," I said without hesitation. "With God there always is hope and He has a plan in mind for our tomorrows."

There were another few minutes of silence; then finally he looked up at me and asked, "Okay, where do I begin?" Then I knew he was ready to start an amazing journey with the Lord—one that if he held to the right course would allow him to experience God's love and provision in a way unlike anything he had ever known. That afternoon, as I closed the door to my study, I wondered how many other people where facing exactly what this young man was facing—a sense of hopelessness and a longing to know God's promise and purpose for their lives.

## *The Discovery*

Discovering God's will hinges on two things: a
desire to live your life for Christ and not for yourself, and your ability to understand the nature of
His will and purpose. These two aspects affect every
area of life. First of all, we need to understand the
fact that God is committed to our success—not in a
financial sense, though He is not opposed to a person making money. He is the one who gives us the
ability to make wealth (Deuteronomy 8:18). His
objection comes when the desires of our hearts are
set on something other than Him. This could
include a material possession or an employment
position. It also includes people, hobbies, and goals
or dreams that simply are not God's best for us. In
fact, anything that takes His place in our lives as
number one is subject to His scrutiny.

The apostle Peter would have understood perfectly what my young friend was facing. When he
first met Jesus alongside the Sea of Galilee, he was
nothing more than a fisherman who had a net full
of dreams and very few fish. Within Peter's life,
Jesus saw amazing potential and, as He stepped up
on the bow of Peter's boat, He surely noticed the

rough intensity that filled His future disciple's eyes. Can you imagine Jesus smiling? I can because He knew the plans He had in mind for Peter just as He knows the plans He has for each one of us.

We should never allow the enemy to stop us at the doorway of opportunity by tempting us to struggle with feelings of doubt and low self-esteem. Instead, we act wisely when we obey God's command just as Peter did when Christ instructed Him to sail out into deep waters (Luke 5:4). Think about it for a moment. Peter was an expert fisherman. Yet, he had been out on the Sea of Galilee all night and had not caught a single fish.

How could he possibly know that God was setting the stage for his call into a ministry that would impact the world with such force that it would never be the same again? Each one of us can probably remember a time when we have argued with God. We could sense the Lord lead us to do a certain thing, call a certain person, or trust Him in a certain situation, but we did not know if what we were hearing or feeling was the right thing to do. Peter was no exception. He was ready to debate Jesus' request and to begin to list the reasons why it was senseless to return to the same place he was the night before. However, at the same time, Christ's request touched something deep inside of him, and suddenly, he had a desire to obey Jesus simply because he knew the One who was doing the talking. The Lord instructed Peter to "move out into deep water and cast his net."

Fishermen with any experience, especially on the Sea of Galilee, knew that fish are caught in shallow water and not in cool and unpredictable deep waters. However, Peter obeyed the Lord's command and it was the best decision he ever made. You will never go wrong obeying God. You may not know exactly where you are going, but you can be sure of one thing: when you get to the place He has called you to go, you will experience a miraculous blessing.

Christ's words to Peter were really not a request. Requests offer options, but Jesus did not offer another plan. He just said, "Put out into the deep water and let down your nets for a catch" (Luke 5:4).

### *The Right Choice*

We can imagine that for a few tense moments Peter's
eyes locked on the Savior's eyes. The sun was beat-
ing down and Peter was exhausted. He had listened
to Jesus teach to those who were gathered around
the shoreline. Deep inside, perhaps, all he wanted
was to go home and fall into his bed and sleep for a
few hours before returning to his boat and work.
Drawing in a deep breath of the sea's air, he nodded
slowly and then agreed to Jesus' command.

Peter's response was perfect and right on track
for an extreme blessing. "Master, we worked hard
all night and caught nothing, but because of Your
instructions I will let down the nets" (v. 5). If you
are looking for the key to Peter's success, here it is:
"Because of Your instructions I will let down the
nets." Obedience always is the first step to discovering God's plan for your life.

Jesus did not step up to Peter's boat and say,
"If you will allow Me to climb on board and speak
to the crowd, we'll go for a boat ride that will
change your entire destiny." Instead, He asked Peter
if He could use his boat. He needed a platform not
only for the miracle that was about to take place,

but He also wanted to speak to the people who had gathered. Wherever Jesus went, a crowd of people followed. These were men and women who were hungry for truth and for a Savior. Peter was among this same group. He longed for Messiah to come just as others did, but at that very moment, he had no idea that the answer to his prayers was now standing within his small fishing boat.

Once his fishing boat was away from the shore, he lifted the sails of the small vessel and headed out for deeper waters. He was living in obedience to God's will and did not even have a clue that this was what he was doing. His simple act of obedience was positioning him for a great blessing.

As he dropped the net over the side of the boat, he probably glanced back to the distant shoreline and wondered what his friends were thinking. *One thing that can block us from fulfilling God's promise for our lives is becoming entangled in what others think about what we are doing.* If God has positioned us in a certain place, we must leave all the details to Him. With total abandonment, Peter obeyed Christ. Imagine the emotion that went through him a few minutes later when his nets began to fill up with fish. In fact, the catch was so large he immediately shouted back to his friends—James and John, who Jesus later called the "sons of thunder"—to come and help him. Then he fell at the Lord's feet and said, "Go away from me Lord, for I am a sinful man, O Lord!" (Luke 5:8).

## *Blessings for Obedience*

Here is the beauty of God's intimate love for you, especially if you have ever been concerned about how He views your life. Jesus responded to Peter in a way that turned his life upside down, "Do not fear, from now on you will be catching men." The New International Version of the Bible says, "You will catch men." In other words, you will catch men for My heavenly Father's glory and no longer be caught up emotionally and mentally with the things of this world.

At the close of the scene, we are left with a memorable image: "When they had brought their boats to land, they left everything and followed Him" (v. 11). It was not the end of the story. Instead, it was just the beginning of God's will being revealed to Peter and those who chose to follow the Savior.

We live in a society that wants instant results—
instant food, instant access to computer programs,
instant service. If it can't happen quickly, we will
usually be tempted to become frustrated and walk
away. If we see something we want, we can find a
way to purchase it. However, experiencing the fullness of God's will is not something that happens
immediately. It takes time—a lifetime. He may give
us an idea as to what His will is, but it takes a life
of devotion to uncover His complete purpose and
plan for our lives. Peter could only handle what
Jesus revealed to him at the moment. There will be
times in our lives, when God will instruct us to step
forward. His express will is for us to obey Him. We
may not understand what He is calling us to do.
However, at this point, His goal for us is obedience. Therefore, we must step forward trusting
Him for the future.

*God has a plan and it should be our goal to live
out that plan to the best of our knowledge and ability.*
Without a doubt, there will be times when we get
off course. Later, we will see how Peter did just that.
However, we'll read how the Lord moved quickly to
get His disciple back on track and back into the cen-

ter of God's will. Many people mistakenly believe that Jesus is too busy to walk with them through difficult times. They forget that He is their ever-present advocate before His heavenly Father's throne.

He prays unceasingly for us. The author of Hebrews writes, "Therefore He is able also to save forever those who draw near to God through Him, since He always lives to make intercession for them" (Hebrews 7:25). When we yield to temptation, Christ is our advocate before God's throne of mercy and grace (1 John 2:1). You may feel as though you do not have a friend you can turn to for help and encouragement. However, you do. Jesus Christ promises to listen to your every prayer and He will never leave you. Instead, He will remain even closer to you than a brother (Proverbs 18:24). This is why we long to fulfill God's will. Once we draw near to His presence and experience His goodness extended toward us, we will want to be with Him every day.

We also will want to spend time with Him in prayer and studying His Word. I often tell people who truly want to know His will for their lives to study His Word, pray, and seek His wisdom for their situations. When we do, He will answer our prayers and reveal the portion of His will that we need to know.

God sees the big picture of our lives and knows all that it will take to get us to a place where we will fulfill His will. He knows how He wants the events of our lives to end. He also knows how to position us so that we fulfill His plan and glorify Him. The purpose of our lives is not to serve ourselves by focusing on what we feel is important and holds value. From God's perspective, this is a very narrow view of the life that He has given you to live. Instead of thinking, "What about me and my desires," the right question to ask is, "Lord, what is Your desire for my life? Please show me Your plan and make Your will absolutely clear so I can do it." Offer the following prayer to God with me.

# CHAPTER TWO

# God's Promise Fulfilled

There is no doubt that God has a plan for our lives, and He wants us to discover it and live in the middle of it. At times, He may reveal to us a portion of His will. We will know that God has brought us to a certain point but not know all that is connected with being there. Remember, Abraham did not wait for God's promise to be completely revealed to him before he obeyed the Lord. Instead, he left his home believing in the One who had called him.

David was anointed king over Israel. However, it was many years before he sat on the nation's throne. These were years of extreme danger and disappointment. He was forced to run for his life from an angry king whose sole existence was wrapped up in ending David's life. Before David could do God's will, he had to be trained by adversity, disappointment, and at times, extreme difficulty. Was he outside the will

of God? There were moments when he made decisions that were not the best, but David kept pace
with God's will even when he could not see how he
would make it through the next day.

Like David, you may be walking through a deep
valley and wonder if you are in God's will.
Remember, He has promised to guide you and lead
you to a place where you will fulfill His will and
purpose for your life. David writes, "Even though
I walk through the valley of the shadow of death,
I fear no evil; for You are with me" (Psalm 23:4).
David was walking through the valley and knew
that he would emerge victorious on the other side
of his problems. He did not become a sorrowful
person. He became a man after God's own heart
and learned to do God's will regardless of his circumstances, and we can do the same (Acts 13:22).

### *Learn to Trust*
David also was the author of a majority of the
psalms, and in Psalm 40, he writes, "I delight to do
Your will, O my God" (v. 8). Then in Psalm 143:10,
his words form a personal prayer, "Teach me to do
Your will, for You are my God; Let Your good Spirit

lead me on level ground." God answered David's prayers and continued to lead him through a lifetime of trials and victories. The question we need to answer is, "Are we willing for God to do the same thing in our lives?"

He has a will for every single one of us and the prayer of our hearts always should be, "Lord, teach me to do Your will." When we pray this way, we are praying the same way Jesus prayed before facing Calvary, "Not My will, but Yours be done" (Luke 22:42). This is a prayer of surrender—surrender to God's perfect will and not our human desires.

Even Jesus, God's Son, understood that God had a plan in mind for His life. While, He did not know all the steps in that plan, He knew He could trust the One who was in control of His destiny. Do you know the same thing? Can you say without a doubt that you are fully surrendered to the Lord so that He can reveal His will in and through your life?

## *Take the First Step*
You may be thinking, "Well, I would take the first step, if I only knew what the plan looked like." Remember, Peter did not know. He just wanted to

obey Christ's call to him. God does not show us
more than what we can handle. He only revealed a
portion of His will to Moses. Then, like David, he
was forced to live years in a wilderness situation that
probably left him wondering if he would ever do
what God had called him to do. The same was true
of Abraham and Joseph. Both of these men were
given glimpses of God's plan for their lives, but they
had to "winter" with God and wait for His appointed time. Timing is everything to God. He knows
the perfect moment to call to you and the perfect
moment for you to answer Him.

When we are willing to listen and wait for His
will, God will begin to unfold His plan and purpose
for us. We know the right steps to take because,
with each move we make, we will sense Him saying,
"Yes, this is what I have planned for your life."

If you have never accepted Jesus Christ as your
Savior, then you do not know how to enter or enjoy
the promise that God has given you (John 3:3). I
can tell you without a doubt that His will for you at
this moment is for you to enter into a personal relationship with Him by accepting His Son as your
Savior. Once you do this, you will be ready to begin

to discover His will along with His exciting purpose and plan for your future.

Before you read any further, take a moment to pray this life changing prayer (John 3:16):

*Dear God, I am so grateful that Your love for me is unconditional and that You have made an eternal promise to me—one that cannot be withdrawn. I realize that You also have an eternal plan in mind for my life and it is one of hope and promise (Jeremiah 29:11). I bow before You and ask that You would save me from an eternal death. I give my life to You and pray for Your cleansing touch over my life and ask that You would place within my heart a deep abiding love for You and Your Word. Thank You that You sent Your Son to die for me on Calvary's Cross. I accept His death as payment for my sins. I also acknowledge my need of a Savior and ask that He would come into my life through the presence of the Holy Spirit. I am grateful that You love me enough to never leave me and that You only desire what is best for my life. Please reveal Your promise to me—the gift You have given through Your Son, so that I may live my life in the light of Your will. I pray this in Jesus' name. Amen.*

## *God's Faithfulness Revealed*

As I was thinking about the writing of this book, God reminded me of a time when He met my needs in a dramatic way. When I was fourteen years old, He called me to preach. I knew this was His will for my life. However, by the time I was seventeen and a senior in high school, I began to wonder how He would pull everything together in order for me to go to college and study to enter the ministry. At the time, the only job I had was delivering papers, and it did not produce enough income for me to save for my education.

Many of the people who read this book can identify with my situation. You know that God has placed a goal in front of you, but you don't know how it will take place. Limited resources and a limited view of the future can leave us wondering if God is really calling us in a certain direction. However, we do not have to wonder when we know in our hearts that He has confirmed His will. At a point like this, the only thing to do is to obey and step forward by faith. This does not mean that He wants us to exercise our faith by using credit cards and borrowing money that we cannot repay.

He is very creative, and He provides for our needs in amazing ways. Often, people come to me and tell me how they know God has called them to the mission field or to preach or to work for Him in another way, but they hesitate. Fear grabs at their minds and hearts and they become stuck in their walk with the Lord. They feel trapped by their circumstances because they haven't caught the vision that God has for their lives. As I turned my situation over the Lord in prayer, I knew that if He had called me to preach, He would equip me for the task. Faith plays an important role in accessing God's promises. Many times, if we doubt His faithfulness and goodness to us, we will miss the blessings that He has for us. Sadly, we also miss doing His will.

As I prepared for my high school graduation, I waited for the Lord to show me what He wanted me to do next. He led me to apply to the college that I wanted to attend. I may have had very little money, but I had a great deal of faith in God's ability. Trusting God to supply all your needs is the key to walking each day in the center of His will.

My financial shortfall was not a deficit because

it did not reflect the infinite resources that are available to all who believe in Christ. At the end of each month, I had enough money to buy the clothes I needed for school and my lunches. However, there was not much left over for anything else. I knew my family could not help me, but I was not discouraged. My youthful faith was set on God, and I was sure that He would open the door that I needed to walk through at just the right moment. I was not wrong.

One night as I finished delivering papers, I stopped to talk with a friend name Julian. I remember it as if it were yesterday. This is how fresh the memory of God's faithfulness to me is. We were standing at the corner of North Main Street and Moffett Memorial Street in Danville, Virginia. Julian was a little older than I was and he listened attentively as I told him that God had called me to preach and I knew that He was also leading me to go to college to study for the ministry. Julian smiled as he listened and nodded in agreement. He asked what schools I was considering, and I began to list several of them.

## *Our Need and God's Provision*

Finally, I stopped and said, "The problem is I just don't have enough money. I can't go to college on the money I make delivering newspapers." I knew that God's promise to me and to each one of us is that nothing is impossible for Him. When He is involved, and we are living life according to His will—that means surrendered to Him and His desires—then He will set up the circumstance of our life so that we are fulfilling His will. I continued to tell Julian that one particular college cost less, but it was not the one that I felt the Lord was leading me to attend.

As he listened I noticed that he had lifted his eyes and was about to say hello to someone who was crossing the street and heading our way. It was the pastor of Moffett Memorial Baptist Church. Before I knew what was happening, Julian and I were wrapped in a conversation with this kind and considerate pastor. I had only been a member of his congregation for a short time. After a few minutes, Julian began to explain my situation to Reverend Hammock. He said, "Reverend Hammock, Charles believes God is calling him to preach, and he wants to go to school but he doesn't have the money that is needed." Reverend Hammock knew I was delivering papers because I was his paperboy!

Julian continued, "He needs some help. Is there any way we can help him?" The elder pastor looked at both of us, thought for a moment, and then said, "Charles, why don't you come to see me tomorrow?" I had no idea what this man would be able to do to help me; but I thought, if he only commits to pray for me, then I know God will answer his prayers and provide the money that is needed. The next day I went to his study and sat down with him. Before I could say a word, he told me that he could get me a scholarship for the entire four years. I was amazed and left his office that day with a smile on my face and a heart full of praise to God.

Some people may think that this was a coincidence, but it was not. There was nothing coincidental about it. God set up the circumstances in my life and He provided the answer I needed exactly when I needed it the most (Ephesians 1:11). He has continued to work in my life in similar ways, and He will do the same for you. In God's eyes, each one of us is just as important as the next person. What

God does for one person, He will do for everyone.
His faithfulness is not limited.

Many times, when a need arises, He may not
answer immediately because He is in the process of
stretching our faith, teaching us to trust Him on a
deeper level, and preparing us to receive His blessings for the future.

The circumstances of your life are extremely
important. Never ignore them because they are
exactly what God uses to direct your life and to
reveal His promise to you. When God is involved, it
is never a matter of luck or good fortune. There is
no such thing as luck in the life of a believer. It is
the hand of God that opens and closes the doors
you face each day. There is no chance encounter—
just the divine moments when God moves to
answer our prayers and accomplish His purposes.

There are three things we need to know concerning God's promise.

• **He will show you His will.** He desires that
you know it and assumes responsibility for telling us
how to live each day in the center of His will. This
is a part of His nature and character. It is, however,
your responsibility to do what He leads you to do.

If He says move forward as He did with Abraham
and Peter, then you need to put on your walking
shoes and move forward by faith, trusting Him to
set up the circumstances of your life and to provide
for the needs you have.

• **He is committed to your success.** He wants
us to live in the center of His will. This is why it is
not a mystery that cannot be found or discovered.
He tells us in Psalm 32, "I will instruct you (give
instruction) and teach you in the way which you
should go; I will counsel you with My eye upon
you" (v. 8).

From our birth, God has been working the circumstances of our lives together in order for us to
fulfill His will. However, because we live in a fallen
world, we often get off track. Yet, God remains
steadfast in His desire to teach us how to fulfill His
purpose and plan for our lives. David knew God
had a plan for His life, but he didn't know all the
aspects of that plan. However, he realized if he
would commit himself to follow wherever the Lord
led him, he would discover it. It would unfold
before him over time and this is exactly what happened. There are times when God places a dream or

a goal in our hearts, and we have to step forward with the intent of reaching that goal. If we say, "Lord, I don't want to move until I can see the whole picture laid out before me, then we will miss not only a great blessing, but we also will miss His will for our lives.

• **He will correct and redirect you when you make a wrong turn.** Many of the people that I talk with have made mistakes in their walk with the Lord. Maybe they made wrong choices that ended up devastating their families. Others have written to say that they felt God was leading them to a certain line of employment, and they ignored His call. Years later, they are fighting feelings of hopelessness as they wonder if it is too late for them to discover God's will for their lives, and the answer is no. His promise is the same as it was the day you were born. God doesn't change; we may, but He is the same yesterday, today, and forever.

*No matter how badly you have messed up, He will take the broken pieces of your life and, with the glue of His unconditional love, put your life back together.* Whenever you turn back to Him, seek His forgiveness, and ask Him to guide you from this point on,

He is quick to embrace you with His unconditional love and forgiveness. He says, "I will take you, right where you are, and show you how to live out the rest of your life with My help and My strength."

## A Crucial Discovery

One of the first things we need to learn is that God is a planner and not a reactor. He planned creation. He also planned for your life. He planned the birth of His Son, the Lord Jesus Christ, and He planned for His death so that we might have eternal life through faith in Him. He planned to establish His people through the local church. He also has planned a heavenly home for us so that we will never be separated from His eternal goodness, love, and mercy.

He has full knowledge of your life, and yet, He designed you for a purpose just as He designed the men and the women of the Bible for their purposes. For example, though he once persecuted the church and witnessed many believers being put to death, God chose the apostle Paul to preach the Gospel throughout the known world.

On the Damascus Road, Christ spoke to Paul and from that moment on everything was different

(Acts 9:1-16). Paul's life took on a new meaning.
Suddenly, Paul's life and everything attached to it
was changed. Once he had been a critical, unbeliev-
ing person, but a few moments in the presence of
the living Lord was all it took to change his eternal
destiny and set him on a pathway that was perfectly
in line with God's purpose for His life.

Maybe, you can relate to Paul's story. He was
older when he met the Lord and had a distinct plan
for his life. However, when Jesus Christ got a hold
of his life, his response was immediately one of ulti-
mate surrender. For years, he resisted becoming a
Christian, and if he had said no to Christ, he would
have missed an eternal blessing. Not only would he
have missed God's will, he also would have missed
the opportunity to be saved, to know God personal-
ly, and to be a part of the greatest mission effort
this world has known.

*What is holding you back from doing God's will?*
Most of us know when God calls to us. We can
sense His presence drawing near because it is unlike
anything we have known. However, if we ignore it,
then God's signal to us grows a little weaker each
time. Finally, it is barely audible in our spirits.

Often people say "no" to the Lord without thinking about the serious consequences of their decision. They resist Him because of their fears and believe that there is no way they can do what He has given them to do. They have failed to grasp the truth and the reality of Matthew 19:26, "With people this is impossible, but with God all things are possible." Finding His will is not difficult, but it does require a deep desire to please the Lord and a heart that is devoted to Him.

## *Honor God with Your Life*

Think about it for a minute. If we had known Paul before he was saved, we would say, "There is no way this man would ever preach the Gospel." The fact was Saul's life did not honor God in any way. However, he made a crucial discovery and that was his need for a personal Savior. Before you can know God's will for your life, you must realize that He has a plan, and the only way you can fulfill it is to surrender your life to Him. Holding back a certain area prevents God from fully blessing you and revealing His will to you.

We may wonder, "Why did Jesus wait so long to

save Paul? Why didn't He approach him while He was on the earth?" Timing is one of the most important aspects of knowing God. He has a perfect time for every event to take place. We may decide that we will go on vacation tomorrow, but God is the one who ultimately holds the reins to our lives in His loving hands. Our decisions are just that, ours. However, decisions that are in step with God's plan and purpose will bring glory and honor to Him. They also will bring tremendous blessings to our lives because we have committed ourselves to obeying Him.

Until Paul met the risen Christ, he was living a life of frustration and self-determination. Nothing is more exhausting than a life fueled by self-energy. *If this is where you are in life, then you could be one step away from burnout.*

Not everyone believes this. Many people believe they can go through life and never worry about God's desire for them. However, if we think about it, from the first moment of creation, God was planning for our redemption. He chose Abraham through whom Christ's genealogical line would come.

Life does not exist so we can think, "Well, I'll just do the best I can and get by some way." God has a purpose in mind for your life, and when you operate within its guidelines, you will excel far beyond anything you could imagine. This is why Paul writes, "We have obtained an inheritance, having been predestined according to His purpose who works all thing after the counsel of His will" (Ephesians 1:11). Just as Jesus Christ is our Savior, we are His inheritance. God has an overarching plan for our eternity, but He also has a plan for our lives and the way we spend our days on this earth.

# CHAPTER THREE

# How Do We Discover God's Promise?

The last thing God wants us to do is to sit around passively hoping everything will work out or come together. Yet many people do just that; they wait for God to open a door and they do little to seek His will concerning their situation. Others know that they are in a holding pattern; but instead of using this pause in life for prayer and praise for what God has done in the past, they get restless and, if they are not careful, can drift in their devotion to the Lord.

Waiting for God's timing requires patience and commitment. Even Joseph, as faithful as he was in his walk with the Lord, had to wait many years for God's plan to unfold in his life. As a young man, the Lord had given him a promise, but he did not see it being fulfilled. Nor did it follow an expected course (Genesis 39).

Because God has a plan for your life, He can take even the most trying set of circumstances and mold and shape them so that you may fulfill His purpose. From our perspective, it may appear that we are way off course, but from God's vantage point, we are following His pathway. Just as He was with Joseph, He is with you and me.

How do we discover God's promise, which is His will and purpose for our lives?

- Through reading His Word
- Through the circumstances of life
- Through godly counsel
- Through listening to your spirit-driven conscience

First, God reveals His will to us through His Word. The saints in the Bible learned to meditate on His Word and truth. They studied His principles and went over the facts concerning how He had worked in the lives of others. As we pray and study His Word, the Holy Spirit leads us to passages of Scripture that fit exactly with what God wants us to do or learn. The Bible is God's primary form of communication with us. We can't live the Christian life apart from God's Word. Once we begin to read it, we will want to continue. As we study its message, we will see God's hand guiding, teaching, and spiritually nurturing us so we will find the right road to travel.

God placed a love for His Word deep in my heart, but He also gave me a desire to teach the truth of His Word to others. My desire was not just to study God's Word for myself; once I was there, I wanted to tell as many people as possible how they could experience true freedom, hope, and unconditional love through a personal relationship with God's Son. All of this is based on His Word and my desire to do His will. What is your deepest desire? Is it to know Jesus first? Or are you battling with feelings and desires that, if left unchecked, could lead you far from God's planned purpose for your life? If this is the case, stop right where you are and tell the Lord about the confusion you are feeling. Confusion is not from Him but from the enemy, whose greatest desire is to prevent you from accomplishing God's purpose for your life.

We were not placed on this earth simply for our own pleasure. God gave us life so that we could enjoy His fellowship and the fellowship of other believers. He desires our friendship and demands our worship. Far too often, however, we have left our posts and gone off to chase other dreams and goals than the ones God has given us.

My prayer is that He would not only become your Lord and Savior, but your purpose for living each day. Once this happens, you will know abundant joy and peace that cannot be shaken.

Second, God reveals His will and promises to us through the circumstances of life. There are times, from our natural perspective, that life may seem out of sorts. We may face a sudden tragedy or loss. Without warning, a husband or wife may come to us and say he or she is leaving. Maybe there were things that we should have done differently, but now, it is too late. Our lives are shattered by our circumstances and the stress feels unbelievable.

We wonder, "How can any good come out of such sorrow?" God never finds delight in our suffering. He is not glorified by evil or the brokenness of our world, but He certainly can do the impossible. What appears to be an ending is really a beginning to Him. Yes, He cares when we hurt. He cried at

the tomb of His friend Lazarus, and His heart cries
even now with us when we are hurting. However,
just as Lazarus rose from the grave, God wants to
resurrect our lives. We may go through a season of
mourning, but it will not last forever (Psalm 51:12;
30:5). When we allow Him to move close to us, He
will heal our hearts and shattered dreams and lead
us on to a spacious place of blessing (Psalm 18:19).

God uses the circumstances of our lives to reveal
His will to us. He also uses them to position us for
a greater purpose and blessing. *What seems to be a
dead end to you today may be God's avenue of hope
tomorrow.* Therefore, you need to be willing to stay
on course and believe that He is using everything in
your life to accomplish His will (Romans 8:28).
There may be times when we are tempted to wonder how we will reach the goals He has given us,
but we will because He is guiding us through the
circumstances of our lives. Every turn we take, every
challenge we face, and every disappointment that
works its way into our lives, is an opportunity for
Him to demonstrate His faithfulness to us.

We may think that we are just going through a
daily grind, but we're not. That so-called daily grind

is leading us to a place and a position where God can bless us and use us in ways that we could never imagine. *Every challenge we face is used by God to prepare us for the next step in life.* We never stop growing and He never stops working in our lives. Even to our dying day, God is working His will out through our lives. I've never lost sight of this fact, even when life became very difficult and I wondered what in the world God was up to in my life. I knew that He had a plan and my responsibility was to stay focused on Him, allow Him to guide me, and be willing to obey Him in every situation. If I did that, He would take care of the details, and the same is true for you.

Jeremiah 29:11 is a verse that we can cling to, not only when we go through trials and heartache, but also when we know that we have taken a wrong turn and need God's mercy and grace. It is a promise that reaches out to us with boundless hope, "'For I know the plans that I have for you,' declares the Lord, 'plans for welfare and not for calamity to give you a future and a hope. Then you will call upon Me and come and pray to Me, and I will listen to you. You will seek Me and find Me when you search for Me with all your heart'" (Jeremiah 29:11-13).

It is hard to stop reading at the end of the above verses. God goes on to say, "'I will be found by you,' declares the Lord, 'and I will restore your fortunes and will gather you from all the nations and from all the places where I have driven you,' declares the Lord, 'and I will bring you back to the place from where I sent you into exile'" (v. 14).

Even when we drift away from God's plan, He keeps His focus set on fulfilling His will in our lives. God never gives up on us. Until we draw our last breath, He is using the circumstances of life to position us to receive His love and countless blessings. Can we say no to God? Certainly, but once we have come to know Him as Savior and Lord, saying no becomes all too painful because our "no" places us on the outside of God's best for us.

The third way God reveals His promise for our life is through the godly counsel of others. Often God speaks to us and reveals His will through the counsel of a godly friend, pastor, or counselor. In Proverbs, He reminds us, "Where there is no guidance the people fail, but in abundance of counselors

there is victory" (Proverbs 11:14). However, we
must always consider if what others say to us lines
up with the Word of God.

Many well-meaning people have given counsel
that is just not a part of God's plan for the other
believer. Often we see this in the lives of those who
are single. They long to be married and openly
express their desires. Loving Christians can push a
man and woman into one another's lives without
considering God's will.

After the vows have been said and the wedding
music has ended, everyone goes home. The couple,
however, must live together forever and, many
times, this is where conflict arises. I remember one
young man telling me that he had met what he was
sure was the "girl of his dreams," and he was going
to marry her. It seemed that his friends knew her
and thought she was a perfect match for him. I
asked him how long he had known her, and he said,
"About a month."

I thought, "There is no way that a person can
truly know someone in that short of a time frame."
I counseled him to give the relationship time to
grow, but his mind was made up. They were mar-

ried, and three months later they were struggling with the decision they had made. Marriage is a commitment and not something we enter into lightly. Be sure when you have a decision to make that you openly seek God's desire. Remember, He has a plan for your life and it could include the person you met only a month ago; but it would be a very wise decision on your part to take time to ask Him to make this clear through His Word and through the peace that you feel whenever you pray.

On the other hand, Paul reminds the older women to instruct and offer guidance to the younger women (Titus 2:3). Regardless of the situation, the counsel we give and receive needs to be godly and something that we know God would approve. If we are unsure about a matter, we need to stop and wait for Him to lead us to the next step. He will and He always does. Be patient and be committed to receiving the best He has to offer for your life. That way, you will never be disappointed.

God reveals His will to us through our conscience. How do we know what is best? We know He has a planned will, but how can we be sure that we have discovered it? When we ask God to make

His will plain to us, He will do it. He has placed
within our lives a conscience, an awareness of His
presence (Romans 1:20). He trains our conscience
with the principles written in His Word. This is why
reading and studying the Bible is so crucial to our
daily walk with God. *If we have taken time to "hide
God's Word in our hearts" then we will have a clear
and firm vision of the hope for the future.*

When tragedy comes, we will stumble and
grope for hope. However, if we have the principles
of God within our hearts, we will know that when
trouble comes we are not alone. We will remember
that His Holy Spirit who lives within us will never
leave us alone. We will also recall the places in
God's Word where He has promised to guide us
and give us the wisdom me need to meet every
challenge (Proverbs 2:6; 9:10; 14:33).

The prophet Zephaniah tells us, "The Lord
your God is in your midst, a victorious warrior. He
will exult over you with joy, He will be quiet in His
love, He will rejoice over you with shouts of joy"
(Zephaniah 3:17). The New International Version
of the Bible puts it this way, "The Lord your God is
with you, he is mighty to save. He will take great

delight in you, he will quiet you with His love, he will rejoice over you with singing." *God actually rejoices over us and loves us with an everlasting love.* We don't have to cower in fear of what will happen tomorrow because God has gone out before us and He had trodden the path that we will walk. This means that He has placed our enemies under His feet. We can walk victoriously through this life knowing that the God of the universe is with us guiding our every step and leading us to places of hope and victory.

Why is it important to understand truth? Because just as God has a plan for your life, Satan would like nothing better than to prevent you from achieving it. He not only wants to discourage the missionary who is faithfully serving the Lord around the world, he wants to discourage the person who sitting right beside you in your office. His goal is to prevent every believer from reaching his or her full potential.

Once you have checked your course according to God's Word and have taken time to "seek His face" through prayer, you are ready to step forward. He will guide you in the way that you should go. This doesn't mean that you will never face difficulty.

In fact, hardship and disappointment are tools that God uses to refine our lives and make His promise for us even brighter.

## *A Word of Caution*

If a person is involved in a legalistic church, then he may have a hard time following his conscience. He knows what God has told him in Scripture. He even can see how God's plan would include certain circumstances. However, his conscience is holding him back because he is afraid that the decision he makes will not be correct. This is because he has grown accustomed to being in an atmosphere where the pastor or a group of leaders tells the congregation, "You must do this or you can't do that." Over time, members begin to think that if they displease the leaders of the church, then God will be displeased. This is a root cause for false guilt—guilt that is not from God.

False guilt creates feelings of anxiety and fear because no one can live up to a set of standards that has nothing to do with the Word of God. People have become paralyzed in their walk with God all because they felt too guilty to trust Him for something greater.

There is another side to this issue. We can become complacent and ignore the warnings of His Spirit. We may think God is leading in a certain direction but we continue to face closed doors. There is a sense of restlessness in our spirits, and it is as though the Holy Spirit is saying, "Don't do it!" However, we continue to push forward anyway. True guilt is God's way of saying, "Hold it! What you are doing is wrong and, if you continue, you will have to bear the consequences of your disobedience."

While false guilt will cause anxiety, true guilt can lead to a greater sense of peace when we heed the warning and stop to listen for God's guidance. One woman was convinced that God's will included the purchase of a new car. Financially, she was not in a position to support this decision. She prayed about it but really did not spend significant time in prayer. Later, she admitted that she had jumped to a conclusion because there was not anything preventing her from doing it.

Many times, God watches to see how we will respond to a situation based on what we have learned in the past. She knew her resources were limited, but she did not listen to her conscience or stop when she felt uneasy in her spirit. Within six months of its purchase, the car had become a huge burden. She started pressuring her employer for a salary increase and complained to co-workers that she did not have enough money to carry her through the month.

Initially, God's warning is very loud and we feel uncomfortable. However, if we continue to ignore it, we will hear it less and less until we cannot hear His words of caution at all.

We are living in a moral climate that is devastating. People do all types of things and justify their actions as being perfectly fine. In fact, many believe that if they do not go along with the crowd, they will run the risk of being labeled socially and politically incorrect. If what others are doing is not in keeping with God's Word and principles, then it is better for us to follow God and not the ways of this world.

I had rather be standing in the middle of God's will, knowing that I am living my life to the best of my ability according to His principles, than living a lie and reaping the consequences of my sin. The apostle Paul tells us, "In the later times some will fall away from the faith, paying attention to deceitful spirits and doctrines of demons by means of the hypocrisy of liars seared in their own conscience as with a branding iron" (1 Timothy 4:1-2). He is not saying that these people will lose their salvation. Instead, he is saying that their consciences will be seared as if they had taken a hot iron and placed it on waxed paper. A seared conscience is deaf and blind to the things of God. Sadly, the person who is living with a seared conscience will miss the joy and the peace that comes from intimately knowing God and doing His will.

*God reveals His will to us through common sense.* Once God has placed His principles in our hearts, He expects us to use our common sense to make wise decisions. We cannot do this apart from knowing His Word and applying it to our lives. Our common sense always should be filtered by the guidance of the Holy Spirit. For example, if a person is deeply in debt and struggling to pay his monthly bills, there is no way God would lead him to borrow even more money, increasing the amount he owes others. Common sense will never lead you in a

direction that is contrary to God's will and principles.  If your common sense is tuned to God's
Word, it will shout a long and strong warning when
we are headed in a wrong direction (Proverbs
23:23).

In Titus, Paul writes, "For the grace of God has
appeared, bringing salvation to all men, instructing
us to deny ungodliness and worldly desires and to
live sensibly, righteously, and godly in the present
age" (Titus 2:11-12). Using common sense does
not mean means that we can do what we want to
do. It is a gift of God just like the conscience that
we use under the guidance of the Holy Spirit. If we
use common sense, we won't drink, smoke, or use
drugs.

On the other hand, our common sense will lead
us to trust God in greater ways. I learned this truth
years ago as a young man. Since that time, God has
challenged my faith on several occasions through the
ministry of In Touch. As we have grown, our ministry outreach has expanded. In the beginning, our
staff was housed in one building, then we sensed
that God was about to take us to another level. We
needed to expand and build a separate building to

house our radio and television equipment, studios, and personnel. However, we did not have the money for a major building project.

Our human reasoning told us the venture was impossible, but our common sense, which was directed by the Holy Spirit, led us to step forward by faith and trust God to provide for the need we had. Months into our planning, a man who had never donated to the ministry called and said that he could not shake the feeling that God wanted him to do something to help our ministry. He asked what we were doing and if we had any special needs.

I told him about our need of a building for the ministry. I also explained that I had found a building and the price was 2.7 million, but I thought I could buy it for 2 million. His response was "I think I can handle that." A few days later, I received his check for the exact amount, and we were able to purchase the building and relocate our entire ministry to this property.

When we place our faith in God and take our hands off the problem, the need, the decision, or the relationship, He will work everything out according to His will for our lives in order to demonstrate His awesome power.

Why did the Lord lead us to step forward and begin planning for this project? The answer is simple: He wanted us to place our trust in Him and not in ourselves. If we had waited until we knew everything would work out perfectly and according to our plans, then we would have been acting in our own strength. Instead, we trusted the Lord for His provision and timing. *God is our source for every need we have, in every situation we face.*

When you are facing a difficult decision, trust Him to provide the wisdom you must have in order to continue toward your goal. You will never be disappointed by placing your faith in the One, who holds the answer to every need you have.

# CHAPTER FOUR

# God's Will Defined

It is not unusual for a young man to come to me and say, "I'm really praying because I believe God may be calling me to preach, but I am not sure. I have been praying about this for some time. How can I know the will of God for my life? Is He calling me to preach or not?"

I always approach this subject carefully, but a good indication of God's will is a desire to move in a certain direction. Therefore, many times I respond, "When you pray about this, if you sense Him leading you and motivating your interest in this area, then more than likely you are on the right course. If He stirs your heart and there is an abiding compulsion in this direction, then this is probably what He has for you."

However, I also add that the way we know for sure that God is leading us in a certain direction is by spending time with Him in prayer. The Lord gives us a strong desire to do His will. This does not mean that all of us should be in the ministry. *God's promise for your life is broad and covers every area of your life.*

He may lead you to become a nurse, a college professor, or a high school football coach. No matter where you are or what profession you have, when your life is connected with His and you are committed to doing His will, then you will know how to live each day. The decisions you make will be in line with what God has planned because your life is surrendered to Him and there is no way that He will not make His will very plain and evident to you.

## *Two Aspects to God's Will*

There are two major aspects to the will of God. First, God has a determined will. Second, He has a desired will. The determined will is God's sovereign, operational will in the world. It reflects how God operates as the Lord of the universe. The Bible tells us that He has established His throne in the heavens and His sovereignty rules over all (Psalm 11:4). The problem is that some people do not believe that He is in control of all things; but if He is not, then who is? Satan is not in control. He has limited abilities that God has allowed to be operational in the world, but he is not sovereign and certainly not in control of God's creation. Likewise, we are not in control of our world or our destinies. God is the only one who has His hand on the controls.

This world did not create itself. Mankind did not begin life as a result of the evolution from a single-celled animal. God created us in His image, and the light of His love lives within those who have placed their faith in His Son, the Lord Jesus Christ. What a marvelous gift we have been given by God—life and breath and enough joy to live each day without feelings of fear or anxiety. The reason? The One who created us watches over us and has promised never to leave us (John 14:16). That is sovereignty and absolute control.

God's determined will is what must be done in this world. It is not up for discussion, nor is it optional. This means that whatever falls within His determined will absolutely, inevitably will happen. His determined will is also immutable. This means it is not going to change. It is irresistible in the sense that no one can ignore it or decide that it will not take place. It also is unconditional.

There are some things that God has done, and will do, that only He fully understands. His determined will is comprehensive, purposeful, as well as unpredictable. For example, in Ephesians the apostle Paul writes, "He predestined us to adoption as sons through Jesus Christ to Himself, according to the kind intention of His will, to the praise of the glory of His grace, which He freely bestowed on us in the Beloved" (Ephesians 1:5-6). In love, He predestined you to the adoption of His Son. This means He drew a circle around your life once you came to know Christ as your Lord and Savior.

Does this mean that some people can be saved while others are not? No. Those who receive Jesus Christ as their personal Savior are predestined to be a child of God forever. Once you have come to know the Lord as your Savior, you cannot lose your salvation. You may walk away from God, but His hand of discipline will follow you every step of the way because He loves you and wants you to return to Him. Can you ever step out of the presence of God? David answers this question for us in Psalm

139, "Even before there is a word on my tongue, behold, O Lord, You know it all. You have enclosed me behind and before, and laid Your hand upon me. Such knowledge is too wonderful for me; it is too high, I cannot attain to it" (vv. 4-6).

## God Makes Known His Will

The knowledge of God is too great for us to know. We may gain knowledge, but apart from God, we really know very little. He holds the world and all of us in His hand. We may think the government is in control of the future, but it is not. God is the One who places men and women in power. He also is the One who removes them. *Without a doubt, He knows exactly what is going to take place and when it will happen.* He is aware of the problems in the Middle East, but He is just as concerned about what is going on in your daily life. He is omniscient—all knowing—and all-powerful. He cares when you are hurting or struggling with a decision and wants to guide you through your difficulty.

Paul tells us God has "made known to us the mystery of His will, according to His kind intention (that is according to His good pleasure), which He purposed in [Christ]" (Ephesians 1:9; emphasis added). There are a lot of mysteries to God's will—events in the past and those to come that we will not fully understand. There will be some things that He shows us and other things that we will not know. Our minds cannot comprehend all the ways of God, but the things that He has revealed to us, we use to discern His purpose in many situations (Deuteronomy 30:16; Acts 2:28).

There is a difference in God's determined will and His desired will. His determined will includes the things in this life that He is going to do regardless of how we respond. It is absolutely indisputable and irresistible. However, the same is not true of His desired will. His determined will happens outside our sphere of control. God says that a certain thing will happen and it does. Period. His determined will includes the things that He will do. His desired will includes the things that He wants to do. *When it comes to His desired will, we have a choice. We can obey or disobey Him.* Included in God's desired will are decisions that we make each day. They may be major or minor choices.

One of the reasons so many of God's people are

not living in His will is because they do not understand it, and they get confused. Then they wobble
through life, hoping that they are on the right pathway. His determined will is very clear-cut—Jesus
came to save us from our sin. God's mercy and
grace were demonstrated through His Son's life and
death. Do we understand how Christ was con-
ceived? We know it was by the power of the Holy
Spirit, but God has not chosen to reveal every
aspect to us.

## *The Step before Us*

When it comes to His desired will, He provides
instruction so we will know what we need to do,
but we must decide to follow His instruction. In
Colossians, Paul writes, "For this reason also, since
the day we heard of it, we have not ceased to pray
for you and to ask that you may be filled with the
knowledge of His will in all spiritual wisdom and
understanding" (Colossians 1:9). This was Paul's
prayer for the Colossian church, and it really is
God's prayer for each one of us so that we might
know and experience His personal will for our lives.

In her book *Candles in the Dark*, Amy Carmichael

wrote, "If the next step is clear, then the one thing to do is to take it. . . . Once when I was climbing at night in the forest before there was a made path, I learned what the word meant in Psalm 119:105: 'Thy word is a light to my path.' I had a lantern and had to hold it very low or I should certainly have slipped on those rough rocks. We don't walk spiritually by electric light but by a hand lantern. And a lantern only shows the next step—not several ahead." When we walk with our eyes set on Christ, then we will do His will.

*A life that is focused on obedience is a life that is lived in the center of God's will.* One of the first things that trainers teach their animals, especially dogs, is to watch them. The command of "watch" is given and the dog learns to stay focused only on its master. Even if there is noise or other activity, the animal must hold its watch. The only person who can break this command is its owner or trainer. The purpose is simple. When the animal is watching its master, it is not distracted.

On a greater scale, if the focus of our hearts is set on Christ, then when we have to make a decision, we will do several things:

- We will turn to the Lord in prayer.
- We will be willing to wait for His answer.
- We will take time to seek His wisdom
  through reading His Word.
- We will obey Him.

## *Trust God above All Else*

It all boils down to a level of trust. Do we trust
God with our lives regardless of what we see, or is
there a shadow of doubt lurking in the back of our
minds? One second of doubt can change the way
we view God's presence in our lives. For example,
many people believe the Bible contains the Word of
God. Here is the error: the Bible does not just contain God's Word to us; it is the Word of God.
Period. The moment you say, "Well, I don't know
if every single word written within it is true" is the
moment you discredit what God has spoken to us
through His Word.

The Bible totally relates to your life and situation right now. It is the infallible Word of God—
written by God Himself, through men who were
His agents or scribes. They were His chosen vessels
to record His principles and plan of redemption for

a lost and desperate world. If you deny even a part
of God's Word, you take a major step in the wrong
direction—a direction that leads far from God's will
and purpose for your life. It is also a direction that
leads along a pathway of doubt, fear, and anxiety.
The results of a single decision as this one can bring
more heartache and sorrow than you can bear,
because apart from faith in God and His Word, you
will begin to drift spiritually. You will lose your
sense of direction because you have tossed aside the
very compass God has given you to keep you on
course and in the center of His will.

However, when we choose to obey the Lord,
we are telling Him that we believe He is who He
says He is. We have a choice to believe or not to
believe. *If we choose to obey and believe, we will come
out a winner every time. It is foolish not to obey God.*

I learned this principle years ago. I was preaching
a revival in Alexandria, Virginia, when I began to
feel God churning something up inside of me. I kept
thinking, "God, I don't know what you are trying
to say to me, but whatever it is, please show me."

After the Wednesday night service, I went back
to my room and knew that God was calling me into

a season of prayer. I wanted to know what God was up to in my life. Many times, when feelings like this come, I take out a legal pad and list what I am feeling or any impressions I have had that could be from God. This night, I drew a circle with five lines coming out from it. On each line, I wrote one of the following—

- Do something unusual in my life.
- Change me in some area of my life.
- Do something in my ministry.
- Move me.
- ?

I placed a question mark on the last line because there seemed to be more but I was not sure what it was. Then I prayed and waited but nothing seemed to indicate that God was ready to reveal His plan to me. However, the next night as I got down on my knees to pray, I instantly knew that God was saying, "I'm going to move you."

## Responding to God's Direction

My mind started to race and I asked, "Lord, when?" Then it was as if a large screen appeared in my mind with the word September written on it. It was April, and immediately I thought, "He must mean next September because I have only been at here in Bartow, Florida, for eleven months." The next night I got down on my knees to pray, but it was as if God had disappeared. He had said exactly what He needed to say and, for the moment, there was nothing else I needed to know.

I came home and told my family what had happened, and we prayed that God would make His will clear. The following Monday a man called me whom I had not talked with for a very long time. After a few minutes of general conversation, he began to tell me why he had called. My thoughts returned to the legal pad and the question mark I had placed on line five.

He wanted to talk with me about a position that was open at his church in Atlanta, Georgia. I was the senior pastor of the church I was at in Florida, but this position was for an associate pastor. I told him that he could probably think of fifty people to recommend for that position. However, he replied that my name was the only one that kept coming to mind.

I assured him that I wouldn't be interested in

becoming an associate pastor and besides, I told him, "I love it here in Bartow." Before we hung up, he asked me if I would be willing to pray about it, and I agreed to do this.

Once I hung up the phone, I burst into tears because I thought, "Lord, what are you doing?"

A couple of weeks later, a pulpit committee from First Baptist Atlanta showed up at my church to hear me preach. I continued to assure them that I was not interested. Every week for the next several weeks someone called to check to see if I had changed my mind, but my answer remained the same, "No." Finally, they asked if they could return for another visit. While I hated to see them waste their time, I agreed. This time eleven people came as well as the senior pastor.

Throughout this process, I could not stop the inner churning that was going on inside of me. I listened as they explained their offer and desire to see me become their new associate pastor. When they had finished, the senior pastor asked, "What is your answer?" I said that God would have to make it so clear to me that there would be no mistake that this move was His will for my life.

The committee left and I began to seek God's face for His will for my family and me. I had never really been to Atlanta and knew very little about the city. On the other hand, I loved the people of our church and enjoyed being so close to the ocean. The word September continued to pop up in my mind. In fact, I could not erase it from my thoughts nor could I stop praying about the move to a new city, even though it would mean that I would not be a senior pastor.

## No Other Answer

Finally, I realized in my spirit that there would be no rest or peace until I accepted the offer. After talking my decision through with my family, I called the pulpit committee at FBA and accepted their offer. The moment I did this, the churning stopped. A footnote to this story is that by September of that same year, my family had moved to Atlanta and I was in my new position. God knew exactly what He wanted me to do and He even revealed the time frame to me. While it was a decision that I did not want to make, it certainly is one that I have never regretted.

Years later as senior pastor to a spiritually strong and growing congregation, I can say without hesitation, if God is leading you to do something, don't resist Him. Get on board with His plan for your life. You will never regret obeying Him. He is the only One who has all the facts, knows all the truth there is to know, and has a wonderful plan in mind for your life. Still the question remains, "Can we know the will of God?" The answer is yes, but in a limited way.

While on earth, even Jesus did not know all that His heavenly Father knew about the future. When questioned about the hour of His return, Christ told His disciples, "That day and hour no one knows, not even the angels of heaven, nor the Son, but the Father alone" (Mark 13:32). While on the earth, there was a limitation to what Jesus knew. He was God in the flesh, but He also was human.

*However, God has full knowledge now and when we ask for His guidance in a particular situation, He will provide it (Matthew 7:7; Psalm 73:24).* Never lose sight of the fact that God's determined will is just that—what He has determined will happen. Nothing can change it. One day, He will

return for those who have placed their faith in
Him. This is an upcoming event and we can rest
assured that it will take place. His goal for us is to
prepare us for the day of His coming by leading
and guiding us through His Spirit into truth and
godly understanding.

In Psalm 25, David prays a prayer that we can
pray each day, "Make me know Your ways, O Lord;
teach me Your paths. Lead me in Your truth and
teach me, for You are the God of my salvation" (vv.
4-5). If you really want to catch God's attention,
ask Him to "teach you more about His ways" as He
guides you each day. He will not resist a heart that
is fully submitted to Him.

# CHAPTER FIVE

# A Miraculous Hope!

*I*f we can know what God wants us to do in a given situation, then what mystery is Paul talking about in the first chapter of Ephesians? Again, it is a portion of God's determined will that He reveals to us. His redemptive plan includes you and me. He planned for our salvation before the beginning of time even though He knew each one of us would choose to disobey Him.

However, through His marvelous grace we are given the opportunity to experience salvation and a new life. Apart from the death and resurrection of Jesus Christ, we would be lost without a single hope. God's Son willingly took our place on the cross and bore our sins so that we might have a personal relationship with God.

The mystery that Paul uncovered is the fact that God has included us in His family. Those who place their faith in His Son are grafted into His family.

The Jews in Paul's day would not accept this fact.
Paul almost lost his life preaching this message.
However, because he did not waver in his obedience but continued to preach the Gospel, we have
this truth to live by each day. Not only are we in a
position to enjoy the goodness of God's love for
eternity, we can also live in the light of His eternal
acceptance as His beloved child. John tells us that
we have been set free from the bondage of sin and
death (John 8:32-36).

There are many aspects of God's will that we
must accept by faith. There is no way to explain all
that He does or will do in the future. This is
because He is God and He is sovereign. He does
not promise to give us total understanding.
However, He promises that if we will obey and
trust Him, we will be blessed no matter what comes
our way. We may or may not understand all that
happens. If you do not, your responsibility is to
continue to obey Him. God sees the big picture.
From His perspective, life is fitting together. Yet, at
times, from our point of view it may appear to be
coming apart.

When many in her family were arrested and sentenced to a Nazi death camp, Christian author and speaker Corrie ten Boom could not understand what God was doing. Her family had sheltered and helped many Jews to escape Poland, but now that she was arrested, who would help her? How could this possibly fit into God's plan for their lives? Yet, no sooner had they arrived at their second destination, than Corrie and her sister, Betsie, began telling others about the Savior's love.

In the book *Prison Letters,* she writes that God placed her "side-by-side with Communists, criminals, Jehovah's Witnesses, Christian Reformed, liberals, and prostitutes." These were just some of the people who began to attend her nightly Bible studies. After her release, she writes about the time she spent at one of the worst camps, "During my confinement in Ravensbruck, where mail was nonexistent, I felt a great emptiness. This was compounded when Betsie became one of the 97,000 women to die there. When Betsie died in camp in the winter of 1944, she left this world with a smile on her face, the smile of one who knows the Savior. She was gone, but I knew she experienced the happiness of Eternity."

"The horrors of Ravensbruck, especially Betsie's death, caused me to wake up to reality. When I did, I was able to see that when all the securities of the world are falling away, then you realize, like never before, what it means to have your security in Jesus. It was not until December 28, 1944, when, through a miracle, I was set free just a week before all the women my age and older were put to death. I was free and knew then, as I know now, it was my chance to take to the world God's message of the victory of Jesus Christ in the midst of the deepest evil of man."

## *God's Plan for a Lifetime*

After her release, Corrie traveled the world telling people about the love and forgiveness of Jesus Christ. She had discovered the will of God for her life through tragic circumstances. However, instead of giving up and sitting on the sidelines of life, she obeyed the Savior's call and thousands of people heard God's truth through this brave and dedicated woman.

Many people stand at a crossroad, and wonder which way they should go. *Never count God out of your plans because He who holds the future also holds your hand*. Like Corrie, when life takes an unexpected turn, you can refuse to become embittered or frustrated because God knows what is up ahead. He can see the sunshine even though, for the moment, you are called to walk through a dark valley. The mystery of God's will is that we have been positioned by His grace to know Him and to live each day for Him. This is His destined will that you will know Him and glorify Him (Ephesians 1:12).

At six-weeks old, Fanny Crosby lost her eyesight at the hands of a man who claimed to be a physician. The grave error left the family in shock and sorrow. However, years later she wrote, "If this accident was a mistake and if perfect earthly sight were offered to me tomorrow, I would not accept it." From her viewpoint, God's will was perfect. During her lifetime, she wrote over nine thousand hymns and witnessed to thousands of people.

You may think that somehow God has made a mistake and failed to keep His promise to you. He hasn't. He has only just begun to work out His marvelous will for your life. In one of her most famous songs, Fanny Crosby wrote:

*All the way my Savior leads me;*
   *What have I to ask beside?*
*Can I doubt His tender mercy,*
   *Who thro' life has been my guide?*
*Heavenly peace, divinest comfort,*
   *Here by faith in him to dwell!*
*For I know whate'er befall me,*
   *Jesus doeth all things well;*
*For I know whate'er befall me,*
   *Jesus doeth all things well.*

## *A Step Further*

Paul takes God's promise of mankind's redemption
a step further and tells us that we have been "sealed
in [Christ] with the Holy Spirit of promise, who is
given as a pledge of our inheritance, with a view to
the redemption of God's own possession, to the
praise of His glory" (Ephesians 1:14). We have a
promised inheritance through Jesus Christ that is
eternal. The Holy Spirit has sealed those who have
placed their faith in God's Son. We belong to Jesus
Christ, and no one and nothing is strong enough to
break this.

   *Life will hold many moments of joy and hope. It*

*also will contain trials and difficulties that will test
our faith in the One who has given us life abundantly.*
Instead of focusing on your circumstances, learn to
watch for God's directive and you will find a certain
kind of peace for your heart and mind that is
beyond anything this world knows.

Can God take your heartache, your trials and
suffering, and even your sin, and turn it into something good? Absolutely! Can He do this same thing
on a worldwide basis? Yes. Is anything too difficult
for God? No.

God's plan for mankind's redemption included
the birth of a son to Abraham and Sarah. The problem was Sarah was beyond the childbearing age. In
fact, she was at least ninety years old (Genesis
17:17). Sometimes, God will allow us to wait for
His will to unfold, but remember, we have said that
God's determined or destined will cannot be
changed. It will take place.

When Sarah overheard God repeat His promise
of a son to her husband, she laughed, and the Lord
asked Abraham, "Why did Sarah laugh, saying,
'Shall I indeed bear a child, when I am so old?'"
(Genesis 18:13). Have you ever felt "caught" by

God when you doubted His promise or instruction? Most of us have, and we also know what it feels like to quench His Spirit through a lack of faith in His ability.

God remained determined with Abraham, but He also revealed a portion of His loving nature and destined will to His servant when He said, "Is anything too difficult for the Lord? At the appointed time I will return to you, at this time next year, and Sarah shall have a son" (Genesis 18:14). The Lord did not have to say another word to Abraham, but He did. His grace is sufficient and His love for us is long suffering. Never give up. You never know just how close you are to fulfilling God's purposes for your life.

Three things can prevent us from stepping into the light of God's will:

• Disobedience. Like Sarah, we get tired of waiting and forget what it feels like to live within the goodness of God's protective will. Instead of waiting, we want to rush ahead or go in another direction, and we suffer as the result of our decisions.

• Setting the focus of our hearts on the things of this world. Remember, timing is everything to God.

He has a set time for the events that will unfold in your life and in the future of our world. Fasting, if it is motivated by our own desires, will not change His mind. His clock is set to heaven's timetable, and we miss a blessing when we think we can convince God to move quicker or change His mind.

• Taking a shortcut around God's planned route. Not only did Sarah laugh at God's reminder of His promise to Abraham, but years before she had taken matters into her own hands. The Middle East remains in turmoil today because of this one decision. Being convinced that God was not going to allow her to have a son, she recruited her maid to have one with her husband. Ishmael's birth set off a firestorm that is still blazing today.

Whenever you are tempted to doubt God's plan or timetable, stop and ask Him to speak to your heart and encourage you as you wait. Don't be afraid to ask Him to draw near to you. He wants you to finish the course that He has set before you. In fact, not only does He want you to finish, He wants you to become a victor in this life. When you set your heart on obeying Him and honoring Him with your life, this is exactly what you will do.

# CHAPTER SIX

# Hindrances to Discovering God's Promise

God calls some people to be pastors, missionaries, and Christian professionals. However, He calls most people to be teachers, engineers, homemakers, doctors, bankers, investors, crane operators, communication advisers, sales associates, technicians, artists, and much more. He gives people gifts, talents, and skills with the sole desire for them to glorify Him and to accomplish His purpose and plan for their lives. Think about this for a moment, where would we be without engineers? We would not have cars, airplanes, trains, or ships, and all of us would be walking. The general rule here is that God has a purpose for your life, and it may be in a profession that is not related to work in the ministry. However, He certainly leads us to be involved in our churches as teachers, ushers, musicians, choir members, committee members, and more.

Regardless of what God has gifted you to do, He also wants you to be aware of the hindrances to fulfilling His will. At some point, you will be tempted to leave your post of service and follow another road than the one He has planned for you to travel. If you are aware of the pitfalls, you will know in advance how to handle thoughts of drifting, disobedience, and ignoring what you know God wants you to do. In Psalm 90:12, we are reminded to pray, "[Father], teach us to number our days, that we may present to You a heart of wisdom."

## *The Danger of Drifting*

Once while my family was vacationing in Florida, my son Andy and I decided to take a couple of inflatable rafts out into the ocean. We had lived near the beach long enough to understand how dangerous ocean currents could be. Before heading out, we placed two markers on the beach just in case we began to drift. We surmised that we could look up and see exactly where we needed to be. We set boundaries, and we knew that if we passed either one of these we could end up going much further down the beach than we planned.

Sure enough, as soon as we climbed on our rafts
we began to drift rapidly past one of the markers.
Without hesitation, we dove back into the water
and swam with our rafts back within the boundaries. This happened several times and, finally, we
realized the current was just too strong, and we
needed to get out of the water.

*God sets boundaries for our lives (Job 26:10).*
These are meant to keep us in the center of His
will. However, if we chose to ignore them, we
could end up drifting away from His plan and purpose. Drifting in our devotion to God is very dangerous. It short-circuits His plans for us and prevents us from enjoying the goodness of His blessing. However, the closer we are to Him, the easier
it is to do what He has called us to do; but many
people fail to do this and sail off in a direction that
is opposite from God's design.

Plenty of people say with a sigh, "I can't figure
out why things don't work out for me." If this
reflects what you are feeling, then take time to be
alone with the Lord in prayer. Ask Him to reveal
His will for your life or even for a certain situation.

He wants you to learn how to discover what He has for you and when you do, you will not be disappointed.

"The secret things belong to the Lord our God, but the things revealed belong to us and to our sons forever" (Deuteronomy 29:29). While there are many things about this life that we will never know or understand—some things are just reserved for the mind of God—there is so much that God wants us to know and understand. However, we cannot tap into these until we have learned to seek God's will for our lives. This means being willing to focus on Him and not just a quick answer or a simple reply.

*Some people believe their lives are so far off course that there is no way they can understand what God has for them.* They struggle with feelings of inadequacy and wonder if He is pleased or angry with them. This is a very frustrating place to be because God wants each one of us to know that He loves us with an everlasting love. His emotions are never directed toward us in anger. We can grieve His Spirit to a point where He becomes very silent and allows the consequence of our sin to entrap us, but

He will never stop loving us. He created each one
of us for a purpose and His goal is for us to live
lives that will glorify and honor Him.

Whenever I hear a person expressing frustration
and fear over not knowing what to do next, I stop
him and tell him that the reason he is feeling this
way is because He is not plugged into God's will.
Or maybe he was, and he began to drift in his spiritual devotion to Christ. *Doubts, misbeliefs, listening
to those who are not living within the will of God, and
many other things can work like a fast moving under-
current to pull us off course and away from God's
plan.* Perhaps, it is time for you to get off the raft
and swim to shore where you can once again have
both feet on solid ground.

## The Danger of Disobeying God

Just as deadly as drifting in our devotion to God is
deciding to disobey what we know He wants us to
do. There is rarely a day that goes by that we are not
challenged to obey God and surrender to His will.

God does not want us to have to face the brokenness that comes with divorce. However, people
get involved in relationships all the time that should

be avoided. They ignore the fact that disobedience builds a wall between God and us. It sidelines us from doing His will and leaves us in a narrow place where we struggle to find enough hope to continue each day.

The woman at the well is a prime example of a life that had been broken by sin, but God still had a plan and a purpose for her to fulfill. Obviously, she had searched for true love and not found it. She had been married several times and was living with a man who was not her husband. From her perspective, her life was at a dead end. Her reputation was so scarred that she could not even go to draw water at the local well with other women. The words of imagined gossip flooded her mind. Therefore, she went alone to the well during the middle of the day. No one but those trapped deeply in sin ventured out in such heat. However, the Savior knew of her misery and the cry for freedom that lay buried deep within her heart.

Maybe, you can identify with this woman's story. For years, you have lived life entrapped by sin and its consequences. You have ended up going through one relationship after another and the person you are now involved with has no intention of marrying you. You feel defeated and find it hard to believe that God would have created you, let alone have a purpose for your life. In fact, you wonder if you prayed to Him, would He even hear your prayers? The answer is yes.

*God never turns away from those who seek Him.* He loves us with an everlasting love. The woman at the well was a seeker. She knew that her father and his father had worshiped God at a certain place (John 4:20). Jesus, however, knew a great deal more about her. He perceived her need for salvation, acceptance, forgiveness, and most of all, unconditional love. This is what God offers everyone who comes to Him. We may think that our sins are too many or too dark to be forgiven, but nothing is more powerful than God's unconditional love. He knows your past, present, and your future and He will not reject you. Instead, He offers you an eternal hope that cannot be dashed.

*He is willing to forgive and restore us.* Jesus asked this woman for a drink of water, but this was just a way for Him to begin the conversation. He knew she was the one who needed the eternal water that only He could provide. She had been thirsty for a long time. Nothing she acquired could satisfy the need within her life. God is the only one who can meet the needs that we have. He created us and in doing so, placed a need within our lives that only He could fill. It didn't matter how many pots this woman brought to the well. Until, she met the Savior and drank from the cup of His eternal love, her life would remain parched and dry.

*He always sets us on a pathway to hope.* Jesus does not leave us comfortless (2 Corinthians 1:3-4). The woman said to [Jesus], "I know that Messiah is coming (He who is called Christ); when that One comes, He will declare all things to us" (John 4:25). We can imagine the Savior looking at the woman deeply as He said, "I am the one who is speaking to you." (my paraphrase of v. 26.) When she heard the Savior's words, her heart probably skipped, and she could not believe what she was hearing.

The Savior, the Messiah, the same God who had counseled Moses and Joshua and Daniel was talking with her—a sinner. Suddenly, the disciples stepped on to the scene and, after giving the woman a stern look, turned to Jesus. The woman, however, left their presence and headed straight into the city where she began to tell everyone what she had heard and discovered. "Many of the Samaritans believed in Him because of the word of the woman who testified, 'He told me all the things that I have done'" (John 4:39).

At times, you may be tempted to think that your life is without hope. This is never the case. God wants you to realize the problem of sin, the consequences of sin, and the sorrow that comes when we disobey God. Ask Him to open your eyes to the truth of your circumstances and be willing to turn away from any and every sin that He brings to mind. Then ask Him to restore you and to place you in a fellowship of believers and a Bible-believing church where you can grow spiritually. Never forget that God created you by His design for a specific purpose. An entire town was saved because of the testimony of one woman whose life was changed through an encounter with the Savior, and yours will be, too.

## *The Danger of Pride*

It was pride that caused Satan's fall in heaven. God had created him and given him a countenance like no other creature. He was beautiful and was the one whom God called to lead worship in heaven, but this position of honor was not good enough. Instead of worshiping the Lord, Satan wanted to be worshiped. Instead of honoring God with his being, he wanted to be honored; instead of submitting to God's authority, he wanted to rule, and rule he has. However, he is not ruler over an eternal kingdom; he is the leader of a doomed regime—one that will see its future destruction in the Lake of Fire (Revelation 20:14).

Pride was the stroke of temptation that the enemy used in the Garden of Eden to lure Eve into questioning and disobeying God. The Lord had given Adam and Eve certain guidelines, but they decided to take matters into their own hands by doing what God had told them not to do. They rebelled against God and suffered the serious conse-quences of their sins. The same is true for us today. The enemy tempts us with words that question God's goodness to us, or with thoughts that cause us to believe we have not received all that should be ours.

*Pride is the opposite of humility and is opposed to the things of God. Judas decided that he knew better than Jesus.* His thinking was very logical but very wrong and not in keeping with God's plan. We can do the same thing in our lives. God had a purpose for His Son dying on the cross. However, Judas wanted Him not to die but to begin an earthly kingdom—one that would include him and the other disciples. His vision was earthbound and limited, and ours can be also.

In a moment of selfish pride, he betrayed the Messiah. Every act of sin is an act of rebellion against God, and it all comes from our desire to lead and not to follow. Pride is a very destructive force. It can lead to personal ruin and deep loneliness. However, you can stop it and prevent it from having easy access to your life. Ask God to reveal to you any pride that you may have in your life.

When Jesus told the disciples that He would be arrested and killed, Peter hastened to stop the Savior from saying more, "God forbid it, Lord! This shall never happen to You" (Matthew 16:22). The enemy's invitation of pride always contains a personal hook—one that is both selfish and not God's best for you.

Jesus countered Peter's statement with a powerful reminder, "Get behind Me, Satan! You are a stumbling block to Me; for you are not setting on God's interests, but man's" (Matthew 16:23). The enemy's ploy always appeals to our flesh and our human nature. However, you do not have to fall for his tactics, nor do you have to settle for a life that is both prideful and isolated from God's goodness and blessing. Seek what God has for you first and then all the desires of your heart will be fulfilled. Not only will you spend your days walking in the center of His will, your heart will be at rest because your life is surrendered to the One who has only your best in mind.

## *The Danger of Ignoring God's Will*

When we think of God's will for our lives, we usually think on a very grand scale—something that is life changing and eternal. However, while the Lord may not have a preference when it comes to what color of tie or shirt we wear for the day, He certainly is interested in every aspect of our lives. He wants us to look our best, do our best, and live in the light of His joy and hope. *God also wants us to learn how to listen for His instruction even in times when we mistakenly believe our situation is small and insignificant.*

I remember once waking up around 1:00 a.m. on a Saturday morning and realizing that I was very sick with a cold. I knew if I did not act quickly, I would not be able to preach on Sunday. As I lay in my bed praying, I sensed the Lord telling me to get up and get some chicken soup. The urge was so strong that I finally got up, went downstairs to the kitchen, and began searching through the cabinets to see if there was a can of chicken soup, but there wasn't.

"God, show me what to do because I can't call the doctor at this hour, and there is no chicken soup in the house." I was feeling worse with every passing minute. Suddenly, I sensed God say, "Where do you get a can of chicken soup?"

I knew the answer—at the grocery store. However, that was not an exciting thought at that hour of the morning, especially feeling the way I did. I knew better than to resist the Lord, got ready, and drove to the store. God's will is not limited to the major matters of our lives. He is interested in all that concerns us. He wanted me to me preach on Sunday, and He also had a plan for my sickness. He would use it to remind me that He was in total control of my life. If I would obey Him, He would give me the strength I needed to preach that weekend.

With this in mind, I drove to the store and bought three cans of chicken soup—one large one and two small ones. I heated the larger can, ate all of it, and then went back to bed. As I lay there talking to the Lord, I began to feel better and, soon, was fast asleep. In the morning, I woke up to a prompting of God's Spirit telling me that the chicken soup had gotten me through the night, but it was not going to heal me. I knew I needed to call the doctor. It is okay to have a cold or sinus problem on Monday, but not on Saturday when I was preparing for Sunday.

By 10:30 Saturday morning, I was sitting in my doctor's office. The next day was Sunday, and I was able to preach—in part because of the medicine the doctor prescribed, but mainly because God intervened and I obeyed His instruction. If I had disregarded God's word to me, I never would have made it to church on Sunday. He places thoughts in our minds that, if we follow, will keep us centered in His will. He wants us to think sensibly, but He is the One, who places the thoughts in our minds.

Likewise, Satan can do the same thing. He places ideas in our minds that are contrary to God's plan for us, and if we are not careful, we will end up following him. He will tell us things like, "Here is an opportunity for you to make a lot of money in a hurry," and we believe him. *We avoid trouble by taking time to be sensitive to the words we hear and by praying and laying the idea out before the Lord.* Ask God to show you who is doing the talking. If it is the Spirit of God, then His words always will glorify the Lord and never contradict His will for our lives or His Word.

## *The Danger of Living Separate from God's Peace*

Some people have lived in an atmosphere of stress for so long they cannot remember what it feels like to be encapsulated with a sense of God's peace. Feelings of anxiety invade their thoughts, and they cannot conceive how they will make it from day to day. However, peace is a gift that God gives each one of us. He tells us to "be anxious for nothing, but in everything by prayer and supplication with thanksgiving let your requests be made known to God. And the peace of God, which surpasses all comprehension, will guard your hearts and your minds in Christ Jesus" (Philippians 4:6-7).

In Colossians, Paul writes, "Let the peace of Christ rule in your hearts, to which you were called in one body; and be thankful" (3:15). Peace is God's umpire. When we have a true sense of peace within, then we know that what we are doing is right in the center of His will. If there is a lack of peace, stop and take time to pray and ask God to confirm His will for your life and situation. Sometimes, you may need to take a step of faith, and then the peace will follow. In fact, the Psalmist writes, "Cast your burden upon the Lord and He will sustain you; He will never allow the righteous to be shaken" (Psalm 55:22). God's presence in our lives is our sustaining peace (1 Peter 5:7).

There will be other times when sorrow or trouble will come, and we will think, "Lord, what am I going to do?" The moment we turn to Him in prayer, a wonderful sense of peace floods our hearts. We don't know how we'll get through the upcoming days or months; but because of His abiding presence in our live, we cannot only get through the difficulty, we go on to receive God's victory because He has promised never to leave us hopeless.

# CHAPTER SEVEN

# Equipped for Every Good Work

No matter what we face in this life—sorrow, heartache, joy, and times of love and laughter with friends and family, God has a plan for it to be used in our lives. We were created to have an eternal mindset. However, before we see this unfold, we must develop our personal relationship with Jesus Christ. I have heard many Christians tell how they could not understand God's will. Many say, "I wish I had understood what God wanted me to do in this situation, or how He wanted me to respond. I feel as though I have missed something that He had for me. Usually, this statement was coupled with a story of regret, tragedy, sorrow, or loss.

We can know how to face life's challenges because God provides the wisdom we need at every turn. Also, we can learn to set goals for our lives based on His will and purpose. Neither one of these are hidden from us, but we must be willing to take the needed time to discover them through prayer, reading and studying His Word, and if necessary, waiting for His timing.

While we may not understand all the reasons God allows a certain incident to happen, or leads us to do a certain thing, we can know that He is at work in our lives. *No matter what the circumstances may be, His goal is to draw us closer to Himself and position us for blessing by fulfilling His will for our lives.*

## Bracing for A Strong Wind

What looks like tragedy to us, over time, will become a tool in God's hand to shape our lives so that we will be more sensitive to His Spirit and to the needs of others. However, one thing we cannot disregard in the process of understanding His will is God's Word. If we ignore the wisdom that it offers, then we will suffer the consequences of making unwise decisions.

The author of Hebrews writes, "Now the God of peace, who brought up from the dead the great

Shepherd of the sheep through the blood of the eternal covenant, even Jesus our Lord, equip you in every good thing to do His will, working in us that which is pleasing in His sight, through Jesus Christ to whom be the glory forever and ever" (Hebrews 13:20-21). God is equipping us to be able to walk with Him on a daily basis and to do the things that are pleasing and honorable to Him. He is also preparing us to do mighty things for Him.

Reading and studying His Word is crucial to our spiritual growth. There is a tremendous amount of peace gained through knowing and even memorizing Scripture. When trouble comes, the Spirit will quicken a verse of Scripture to our minds. Or perhaps, when we just need to be reminded of God's unconditional love for us, He will bring to mind a verse that is personal to us and to our relationship with the Savior. He encourages us the same way.

You may be praying about a certain need and just don't know which way to turn. Then you remember a certain portion of His Word and think just how much that means to you as you deal with your current circumstances. You didn't just "happen" to remember this Scripture, the Holy Spirit brought it to mind so that you would be encouraged and would keep walking in the correct direction. However, if you live life through the eyes of your own human reasoning, you will not experience a deep inner peace because you will always wonder, "Am I on the right track? Am I living in God's will?"

*Storms will come and winds will blow hard against your life, but when the entirety of your life is wrapped up in Jesus Christ, you will feel little more than the push of a gentle wind.* However, far too often, when tragedy strikes, we will cry out wondering if God sees or understands our plight. He does, but He may be waiting to see if we will trust Him or cower in fear. He also wants us to learn that He is in full control of the circumstances surrounding our lives.

## *Over to the Other Side*
The disciples learned this lesson out on the open Sea of Galilee, which is known for its sudden outbreak of storms and high winds. After a long day of teaching, Jesus instructed His disciples to get into a fishing boat and go to the other side of the lake (Mark 4:35). God had a plan in mind even for this

venture. Christ's followers could have caught on to the fact that they would not die along the way because the Son of God already had said, "Let us go over to the other side." But they apparently missed this part of the discussion. When the wind started to pick up, they realized a storm was approaching.

Most of the men on board the boat were seasoned fishermen. Peter, John, and James especially should have known how to deal with this type of weather, but the storm that hit their boat was so fierce that they were frightened beyond anything they had experienced. They began to cry out. Jesus, however, was in the stern of the boat lying on a cushion sound asleep. The promises of God lived within His heart and He was not afraid. His followers had the Son of God with them—the promise of eternal hope and salvation—and yet, they did not grasp this fact and became overwhelmed by fear.

Finally, one of them woke Him and said, "Teacher, do you not care that we are perishing?" What a question to ask the Savior, the One who already had said, "We're going over to the other side."

Are you traveling through a difficult time in your life and wondering if you will survive? These men did, but you don't have to wonder or ask, "Lord, do you care?" He cares with an eternal love—one that has protected you and watched over you all of your life. When difficulties come, when you don't know the right decision to make at home or in your work, you can turn to the one Person, who has given you a promise and know that you will make it over "to the other side."

Jesus stood up and, more than likely took a moment to take stock of His bewildered team of frightened disciples. Then with all the power and force of heaven at His disposal, He rebuked the wind and said to the sea, "Hush, be still." Mark tells us that the "wind died down" and the sea became "perfectly still" (Mark 4:35-39). Then Jesus turned to them and asked, "Why are you afraid? Do you still have no faith?" (v. 40).

## Faith in God Is the Key

One of the requirements of discovering God's will is faith. It takes this to uncover what He has planned for you to do. It also takes faith to hold the right course when the winds of adversity blow hard against your heart and mind. This is why it is so important to know God's Word and to pray, asking for His guidance each day. If the disciples had taken time to think clearly, they would have realized that they were in the company of the Savior, and He was not about to abandon them or His plan for their lives. Be encouraged when difficulty comes because either you are on the right path or God is in the process of making a course correction in your life. Either way, when you submit your heart and life to Him, you will continue to advance and come away with a great blessing.

Many wonder how God can be glorified through the tragedies of life. If we truly trust Him, He will provide the peace and understanding we need to settle this issue. *We live in a fallen world where bad things happen. However, God is infinitely good, and He has the ability to use our brokenness and sorrow for His glory and for our good.*

The apostle Paul writes, "We know that God causes all things to work together for good to those who love God, to those who are called according to His purpose" (Romans 8:28). God works all things together for good, but there is a condition to this promise and it is this: we must live our lives devoted to Him. He loves us with an everlasting love, but He also desires our devotion and love in return. The will of God is wrapped up in our relationship to a loving God, who only has the very best in mind for each one of us.

When our world seems to fall apart, He is near to our hearts holding the eternal glue that prevents us from caving into hopelessness and sorrow. Certainly, we can live life in a way that overcomes any obstacle because of His power within us. But what happens when we are living outside the will of God—when we have turned our backs to His plan and purpose? Two things that become very apparent are our lack of joy and lack of spiritual discernment.

"The golden rule for understanding spiritually," writes Oswald Chambers in *My Utmost for His Highest,* "is not intellect but obedience. If a man wants scientific knowledge, intellectual curiosity is his guide; but if he wants insight into what Jesus Christ teaches, he can only get it by obedience."

Chambers goes on to write, "If things are dark

to me, then I may be sure there is something I will not do. Intellectual darkness comes through ignorance; spiritual darkness comes because of something I do not intend to obey." Obedience is a key to finding God's will for your life. The moment you say, "No, Lord, I won't do that," is the moment that you miss out on a tremendous blessing because you have taken a step away from His will and one toward disobedience.

## *God's Glory—Our Good*

It is easy to overlook the awesomeness of God's grace, especially for a person who has spent a life battling sin or some addiction. The person involved may not be able to conceive how God could love him, let alone have a plan for his life; but He does. From His perspective, there are no hopeless causes. The wonderful truth about God is that He loves us. Period. In fact, He loves us so much that He sent His Son to die for our sins.

You may feel discouraged and as if you have wasted your life, but let me assure you that you have not. Even at the age of sixty-five or seventy-five or even older, God wants you to know that He

loves you and still has a plan for your life. Though
you may have spent years separated from Him, the
moment you return or ask Him to save you, He
does and your new life in Christ begins.

You may be thinking, "Can God really be glorified through sin and disobedience?" The answer is
yes. He doesn't want us to spend our lives
entrapped or enslaved by sin. However, when we do
yield to temptation and disobey Him, He will not
remove His love from us. He created us with a
design and plan in mind, but in order for this to
take shape, we have to decide to yield our lives to
Him. Once we do, He will position us to know a
portion of His plan. We take one step and then He
leads us on to another.

*Step by step, we follow the Savior to a place of
blessing, hope, and inner peace (Psalm 29:11)*. We
are never too old or too young to begin this
process. The prodigal son made a horrendous mistake, but his father did not abandon his love for his
son. Though he was sure he could live a life apart
from the comforts of his father's home, he soon discovered just how wrong and foolish he was.
However, this did not happen before he asked his

father for his entire inheritance. Once he received it, he headed for the city where he promptly began to waste it by living a lifestyle that was destined for one ending: sorrow and heartache.

After the money was gone, the son quickly realized what he had done and how he had fallen prey to his own selfish desires. He was not living his fantasy; He was living a nightmare! Suddenly, he knew he had no place to turn. The only job that he could find was one of feeding pigs. After days of filling pig troughs with food that was better than what he had to eat, he came to his senses and decided to return to his father's house. He thought if he could be a servant then he would be better off doing that. We must realize that, as long as he was living outside of God's will, the blessings he once knew were cut off. However, once he gained a servant's heart and mindset, the blessings returned and increased.

### Nothing to Gain Apart from God

There is nothing to gain living apart from God's will. We certainly can't humanly discern His plan and on our own, we become lost and very lonely

even if we are in a crowd of people. In fact, you
can have dozens of friends, but if there is a wall
between you and the heart of God, then you are
going to feel lonely and, more than likely,
depressed. This young man's display of humility
and confession brought glory to God. Did he step
out of God's will? Yes, but God provided a way for
him to experience complete restoration. Jesus told
this story with one goal in mind: all of us, no matter what we have done or where we have been, can
come home to our heavenly Father. There is no
place you can travel that is too far from His love.

You can read the full story in Luke 15. However,
the part people seem to enjoy the most is when the
father races out to meet his returning son. Perhaps,
it is because all of us, at some point, have longed
for the Lord to race out to meet us. We have all
failed and sought His forgiveness and restoration.
This young man probably thought for certain that
he would be scolded and forced to live in the quar-
ters set aside for those who worked for the family.
Instead, the father called for the best robe to be put
on his son and then for a "fatted" calf to be killed
and cooked in honor of his son's return.

Sin has consequences. Without a doubt, stepping out of God's will and away from His plan will bring heartache and regret. However, the moment you turn back to Him and say, "Lord, I was wrong. Can I come home?" He rushes out to meet you and gathers you up in His loving arms.

*The valley you walked through may have seemed tremendously dark. However, it was necessary to accomplish His loving will in your life.* Even though you wondered if you would come out on the other side, God knew you would. He also knew that He would be waiting for you and would rush out to meet you and to tell you that He loves you.

Someone may say, "Well, is it okay to sin so God is glorified?" The answer is no. God wants us to live lives that are holy and pure before Him. He tells us to be holy because He is holy (Leviticus 11:44). However, when we do sin, He has a plan in mind for our restoration—one that will ultimately lead us back to Himself.

## An Infinite Promise

Remember, He has promised that He will never leave us. It may appear that we have left Him, but

we are never really out of His sight—just out of His
will. Sooner or later, our actions will catch up with
us and when they do, we must decide whether to
return home or keep running. There are people
who run away from God their entire lives.
Exhausted and full of anxiety, they no longer
remember what decision led them away from their
first love, the Lord Jesus Christ. All they know is
that running keeps them from thinking about
tomorrow and the day after that.

*One step of obedience stops the racing of our
hearts.* We may have to face the consequences of
our decisions, but we can come home. When we
do, a deep, abiding peace returns, and we know
that we are, once again, walking in the center of His
will. The best part of our restoration is that He puts
us to work. Waiting around with nothing to do can
breed feelings of insecurity, depression, and fear.
The first thing the woman at the well did was to go
into the city and tell people about the Savior. "The
woman left her waterpot, and went into the city and
said to the men, 'Come, see a man who told me all
the things that I have done; this is not the Christ, is
it?'" (John 4:28). The New International Version of

the Bible records the last part of that sentence this way, "Could this be the Christ?"

When news spread concerning Jesus, most of the town hurried out to meet Him. John records, "Many of the Samaritans believed in Him because of the word of the woman who testified" (John 4:39). *God's will is for us to point people to His Son.* The moment we turn to Him and acknowledge our need for Him, He meets the needs of our hearts.

He also places us in a position where we can tell others about His saving grace and matchless love. How can we do this? Just like this woman, we have experienced it first hand; and while sin is never a good option for a believer, when we fall into its grasp and then step away from it, God is determined to restore us, give us hope, and set us on a road to service in His kingdom. To know and understand the will of God, you must come to a point where you realize that from God's perspective, there are no hopeless causes—no one beyond the reach of His infinite love. We can choose to deny Him, but He will never stop loving us.

## Saying No to Temptation

Satan is the one who enjoys bringing destruction to our lives through the temptation of sin. He longs to lead us to a distant country by telling us that there is a better way to live than the one that God has planned for us. This is exactly what he did in the Garden of Eden, and it is portrayed in the story of the prodigal son. The enemy tempted Adam and Eve to question God's authority and will for their lives. They believed his lie and ended up losing their home and place in paradise.

However, God had a plan. He knew the decision they would make. As He walked through the garden that evening looking for them, they really were not hidden from His sight. At that moment, His determined will for mankind's redemption began to fall into place. He provided clothing for them by slaying the first animal. This one act set into motion the coming of Christ hundreds of years later. It foreshadowed His sacrificial death for you and me. We never have to question God's goodness to us because, at every turn in our lives, He is present leading, guiding, and providing for us.

You may be thinking, "I can never know God's will. It just seems overwhelming and impossible." You can. The woman at the well stopped and listened to the Savior. She was right where she needed to be. From that moment on, her life changed dramatically. Suddenly, she had a purpose. She could open her heart up to the dreams that God had for her. For years, she had been in bondage and now she was free to really love and be loved. For the first time in her life, she was not struggling to be anything other than what God made her to be.

# CHAPTER EIGHT

# *God's Will Is Clear*

*I*n order to experience this level of freedom and peace, we have to learn to be sensitive to His presence and listen to His word spoken to us. When my children were young, they often wanted to know what I thought they should do in certain situations. One day, I remember being in my study and looking up to see both of them standing in the doorway. It was obvious that they wanted to ask me a question. Finally, one of them told me what they wanted to do and asked my opinion. I knew what was right, but I wanted to see what they would do; so I told them that they should pray about it and see what God had to say.

They both chimed in and said, "Aw, Dad, you always say that. We want to know what you think we should do." For a moment, I was tempted to answer their question but decided against it. God wants us to learn how to seek His wisdom for our lives—no matter how young or old we are. The easiest thing for me to do would have been to say no, or yes, or even maybe, but I wanted them to learn that they could go to God and He would provide the right answer. One of the most important things parents can do is to teach their children to spend time with God asking Him to show them His will for their lives. Then when they are older with their backs against a wall and a decision that needs to be made, they will resist the temptation to make a decision based on their own knowledge. Instead, they will ask God to make His will and way perfectly clear.

Later, that same day, they reappeared in my study. This time they were all smiles and announced that they knew what God wanted them to do.

I said, "Alright, let's have it." Without batting an eye, they launched into telling me what they had concluded, which was the opposite of what I knew God really wanted.

They said, "He told us to do (a certain thing)," and I said, "There's no way He said that. Now, go back and ask Him again, but this time ask Him to confirm it to you in His Word."

Their faces dropped because they were both old enough to know that God's Word did not contain the answer they were looking to find. Another hour or so passed and, when they came to me, the look on their faces was not as bright; but I could tell they had accepted the fact that they were not going to go through with their plans. In fact, as we talked, they admitted that God had confirmed to them that they were off track and headed for trouble.

## *A Life-changing Discovery*

*When we rely only on human knowledge, we end up getting into serious trouble.* Always take time to ask God to show you the direction you need to take in life, and expect Him to answer in one of three ways: yes, no, or wait. This is how you discover His will.

We always realize that He is the One who places His dreams in our hearts. If we are drawn to a certain vocation or sense God calling us to do something that we have never dreamed possible, it could be that He is the One who is leading us and turning us in a direction that will one day glorify Him. When Jesus called Peter and John into the

ministry, they were fishing on the Sea of Galilee.
They had done this all their lives. However, deep
inside of them was a hunger to know God. They
longed for Messiah to come, and when they heard
the Savior speak, something within their hearts and
minds were drawn to Him. They did not know
what it was. They had never experienced God's
personal presence. Once they did, they were ready
to leave everything in order to be in the middle of
His will. Think about what Jesus said to them
(Matthew 4:18-22).

He never wants us to be confined to a day in,
day out existence. Instead, He wants us to learn to
live on the higher planes of life where His blessings
are and where we can glorify Him more each day.
Will there be valley times? Yes, but even in the dark-
est valley, God lights a lantern of hope for those
who believe and trust Him. He is interested in
every aspect of our lives.

He may not care if you wear black socks to
work or gray ones, but He certainly cares how you
handle the events of your day. He has a broad overarching plan, and then He also has a desired will for
you to fulfill. Along the way, we make countless

decisions. In fact, each day, the decisions we make often have the ability to keep us focused and on course, or set us on a pathway that will lead us to a place of disobedience.

## *Let God Handle Your Life*

Moses' desire to see God's people set free ended up costing him forty years in the wilderness. We can imagine that after this length of time, his goal to be "the deliverer" had started to fade. However, once this happened, he was in a position to be molded and shaped by the hand of God. Many times, we cling to our desires and dreams, not realizing that they are preventing us from experiencing God's best.

Just as the Lord had chosen Abraham, He chose Moses for a particular task. But Moses wanted to do it his way, and this was a problem. He was not ready to assume the responsibility God had planned for him until he had been broken by spending time in the desert. *When we try to push ahead of God, He has no option but to place us in a position where we have to wait for Him to lead us on to the next point.*

In a moment of rash behavior, Moses ended up

killing an Egyptian official. Most of us would think
that this would be the end of the story, but it was-
n't. Many of us have failed to follow God's will and
ended up sinning against Him. When people ask if
sin was a part of God's plan, I realize that they have
not considered the sovereignty of God. They think
there is no way that sin could be a part of God's
design, but they fail to realize that God is not surprised by our sin or disobedience. He knows what
we must face in order to be prepared for service in
His kingdom. He doesn't initiate sin, but He certainly uses it as a tool to model and shape our lives.

In Ephesians Paul writes, "[God] chose us in
Him before the foundation of the world, that
we would be holy and blameless before Him.
He predestined us to adoption (to make us His
children once we trusted Him as our Savior) as
sons through Jesus Christ to Himself, according
to the kind intention (or good pleasure) of His
will" (Ephesians 1:4-5).

What did God choose us to do? He chose us
to be holy and blameless. If sin was not a part of
God's plan, then we need to ask the question,
"Did God make a mistake and just react in the

Garden of Eden?" Did He say, "Let's fix this quick?" No, He knew that sin would be a part of the equation and that the problem could only be solved by faith in His Son, the Lord Jesus Christ.

## *God is our Redeemer*

Moses' wrong reaction to a situation only made matters worse. God had a plan in mind, but Moses didn't read the fine print. He acted on his own intuition and authority, not God's. The day and time of Israel's deliverance was not up to Moses. It was God's to decide. However, Moses wanted to hurry things along. In righteous indignation, he acted without the Lord's direction and ended up sinning against Him by committing murder.

If you ever have wondered whether God can use you after you have bitterly failed, the lives of Moses and Abraham should settle this issue. God uses those who make their lives and hearts available to Him. His determined will for mankind is one of redemption. Part of His desired will for your life is for you to live completely devoted to Him.

While He does not want us entrapped by sin, He certainly forgives and restores. We also need to remember that He knows the plans He has for us (Jeremiah 29:11). You can get off track, but this does not change God's determined will. You can take a wrong turn and end up in a place in life that seems as though you are living in a very distant land. God will allow you to come to the end of yourself. More than likely, this is what He allowed to happen in Moses' life. He knew that Moses could not be used to fulfill His purpose until he had been broken by the circumstances of life. If you are going through a time of brokenness, then know that you are on your way to a great blessing. God breaks us in order to use us for a greater purpose.

God positioned Moses in a safe place—away from the temptations of an Egyptian lifestyle. From our perspective, it may have appeared that he was in isolation, but he was in God's training camp being prepared for his role as Israel's deliverer. When it was time for him to enter God's service, the Lord set a bush on fire and Moses' heart focus was drawn to it. This is when God spoke to him. "When the Lord saw that [Moses] turned aside to look, God called to him from the midst of the bush and said, 'Moses, Moses!' and he said, 'Here I am'" (Exodus

3:4). The moment we say, "Here I am, Lord," is the moment we position ourselves to do His will.

## Four Principles to Guide Us

There are four aspects to God's desired will:

**• He wants us to obey His moral laws.**
For example, He wants us to obey the Ten Commandments and to live according to the Sermon on the Mount (Exodus 20; Matthew 5-7). We are to love one another, forgive one another, and remain faithful to one another. The greatest commandment, however, is to love the Lord our God above everything and everyone else. When we put God first in our lives, then we will see His will unfold before us. Those who seek Him and obey Him are the people who learn to listen for His still small voice. They watch for His ways to open up before them, and they are patient in their love for the Savior and others. There is no demanding of personal rights. Instead, there is surrender to God for His is good.

In 1 Thessalonians 5:18, Paul reminds us to be thankful, "For this is God's will for you in Christ Jesus." When we praise and thank God for His goodness toward us, the focus of our minds and hearts changes. We are no longer focused on what went wrong or our feelings of inadequacy. Instead, our hearts are set on Christ. When this happens, He is free to work in our lives in miraculous ways.

Another moral law that God wants us to follow is forgiveness. Paul writes, "Do not grieve the Holy Spirit of God, by whom you were sealed for the day of redemption. Let all bitterness and wrath and anger and clamor and slander be put away from you, along with all malice. Be kind to one another, tender-hearted, forgiving each other, just as God in Christ also has forgiven you" (Ephesians 4:30-32). Imagine what would happen if we truly practiced God's moral law of forgiveness. We would forgive without any thought of retribution or anger. This is exactly what God calls us to do: forgive others because He has forgiven each one of us.

We do not have a legitimate right to be unforgiving toward anyone, no matter what he or she has done. When we forgive someone for a wrong that has been done toward us, we are acting like Christ. It does not change the fact that the person was wrong. We are simply releasing the entire matter to

God. Then we are free to live without bearing the burden of unforgiveness. At times, we may feel as though we have been crucified, but we haven't been. Jesus, however, was crucified for our sins, and He has forgiven each one of us.

• **He wants us to focus on the vocation He has chosen for us.** God has certain intentions for your life. He wants you to discover the vocation that He created you to do. In fact, He has chosen an occupation that fits your skill, ability, talent, personality, and spiritual gift. He gave each one of these to you before you were born. He will never place you in a position that you are not equipped to handle. If He leads you into a certain career, you can be assured that He will equip you to handle it.

You may think about a certain job and decide that there is no way you can do it, but God has placed His dream within your heart. Over time and as you pray about it, begin to imagine what it would be like to have that certain position. This is when you actually realize that God is leading, and if you will follow Him, you will experience a great blessing.

God's desired will is intentional. He has a plan for the way you handle your finances, your relationships, and your vocation. However, you also have a limited free will. If you choose not to follow His guidance, then you will keep repeating the same lesson over and over again until you come to a point where you see that His will is a clear path—you have just been walking along another road.

• **He wants us to learn from our mistakes.** One of the smartest things we can do is to pray and ask God to help us learn from our mistakes. However, many people fail to do this. They make one mistake, and instead of resting in the Lord, their minds tell them to hurry up and make another decision. They do and find that it was worse than the first one. This frustrating cycle goes on until, finally, they are exhausted and broken before the Lord.

For example, one man told me that he did not believe God cared whether he was in debt or not. I said, "Oh, yes, He does. God doesn't want you worrying and fretting about how you will pay the next bill. He has a plan for your life, and until you deal with your debt, you can't do it. There's a blockage and it has to do with your finances and the way you handle the assets God has entrusted to you."

Those were the last words this man expected to hear, but what I said was true. When we are bound by anything other than the love of God, we cannot do what we were created to do for Him. Each one of us has made many mistakes. We have sinned against God and stepped out of His will at some point. The truth is that many people grew up not knowing that God had a purpose for their lives. They tried to do the best they could and ended up making one mistake after another.

How does God respond to the wrong turns we take? First, He leads us to a point where we realize we have made a horrendous mistake. When we confess our sin and foolishness to Him, He forgives us. Second, He takes the pieces of our broken lives and puts them back together. From that point on, we begin to walk through life in the light of His awesome love. When the prodigal son came home, did the father say, "You disobedient, immoral, wasteful son: you messed up your life"? No, here is what he said, "Bring me the robe of honor, a ring for my son's finger, sandals for his feet, and kill a fatted calf. We are going to have the biggest party because my son, who was lost, has come home" (Luke 15:22 my paraphrase).

Do you believe the father placed his son on the lower end of his property to live? No, he did not; once a son, always a son. God picks up the pieces of our lives and puts them back together. Then He says, "From this point on, this is My will for you. You may think that your life is over and there is no hope for you, but nothing could be further from the truth." God is a restorer and He will pattern your life according to His will. His desire is that you will never drift in your love for Him because He knows that, if you do, you will yield to sin and step out of His will.

However, when you turn back, He meets you with open arms of love. His will may take on a different set of circumstances, but it will continue from that point. He takes you where you are and teaches you that He is your Savior and that He is not ashamed of you. I urge those who have fallen because of sin to "march forward" knowing that God will take the years they have left and make them fruitful and productive. They are not sinners. Their names have been written in the Lamb's book of life and they have a home in heaven and a great reward.

• **He wants us to listen for His voice and to heed His warnings.** For no apparent reason, God may urge you to turn left at the next traffic light. You think this is a totally ridiculous thought until you continue driving straight ahead and are hit by a car turning into the intersection. There are many times that God warns us not to do something, but we push forward thinking that we know what is best. Perhaps, He cautions us not to go to a certain movie or engage in an activity that others are doing. Instead of heeding His warning, we ignore Him and usually are very sorry we did not listen to what the Spirit was saying. We can come to a point where we barely hear His voice because we have ignored Him over and over again. He is not going to choose the color of socks you wear in the morning, but He does care deeply about many of the countless decisions you will make during the day. (Psalm 139:24)

The best way to handle this is to get up in the morning and ask Him to guide you according to His will through the important events that you will face. Pray without ceasing was Paul's word to the believers. When our hearts are attuned to His Spirit, we will follow where He leads. Abraham sensed

God telling Him to leave his home. He did and received God's greatest promise. As a boy, Samuel heard God call to him. He answered knowing that he could trust the One who called to him.

God has something very special for your life. He has a plan and He wants to reveal it to you, but you must be willing to listen for His voice and then to obey Him. When you do, you will discover not only His will and purpose for your life, you will experience a personal, intimate relationship with the Savior—the only Person who can lead you on to a place of eternal hope and infinite blessing.

# CHAPTER NINE

# The Discovery

Years ago the ministry of In Touch was just getting started. We were still in our downtown Atlanta location and trusting God to provide new cameras for our television program. This was the first major purchase we made and it truly was a step of faith. Even in the early years of our operation, we sensed that God was leading us to do something that was beyond our ability. This always is true when we come to a point of living in His will.

He will place a goal or challenge before you, and then He will give you the desire to reach it. As our church congregation grew, so did our television audience. Every week, we received hundreds of letters telling how God was using the In Touch broadcast to change lives and motivate people to develop a personal relationship with Jesus Christ. I was encouraged and believed that we were walking right in the middle of God's will.

## *A Walk of Faith*

However, I also realized that this would be a walk of faith. Many times, God only tells us what we need to know about His will when we need to know it. Other times, He may reveal several steps that are a part of His plan. Regardless, our duty is to respond to Him in faith. When He says step through this door, then you need to step through it. However, if you sense Him saying wait, then you would be very wise to wait and not move ahead. Moving forward without God's leading often leads us on an off-road detour. In other words, we get off track and head in a direction that is not what He has planned.

*Walking in the light of God's will is a journey of faith and love.* Our love for Him must become so great that we are willing to walk each day believing that wherever He leads, we will find blessing and hope, and that we will also end up in a place where He will use us greatly for His kingdom work.

With this in mind, we began to ask the people of our congregation to pray for God's wisdom, as we trusted Him to provide the money we needed to purchase new cameras. I was especially motivated and felt challenged to ask our members to contribute, since many had expressed a desire to see our program grow and become available to television outlets around the world. Therefore, we set a Sunday aside for God's people to give toward this goal. However, I had no idea that I would not be preaching on that day due to an illness. I was prepared to preach and certainly looking forward to seeing what God was going to do. However, I could not get out of bed and this is when I asked the Reverend Ian North to preach on that Sunday in my place.

Was it God's will that we go forward and trust Him for the money we needed? Absolutely! Did God have another plan in mind other than the one I thought was unfolding on that particular day? Evidently, He did and that is God's right—He can alter a portion of our course, and we will continue to be right in the middle of His will. He doesn't have to tell us why or give us any explanation. *A major part of understanding and discovering God's will is to trust the One who is leading us.* Remember, "By faith Abraham, when he was called, obeyed by going out to a place, which he was to receive for an inheritance; and he went out, not knowing where he was going" (Hebrews 11:8).

## *God Knows the Way for You to Travel*

God knew exactly where he was going, but Abraham only knew that God was calling him to "go." He had enough light to see the steps he needed to take immediately in front of Him, and there will be times when this is all that God gives us. What do we do? We step forward and trust Him to reveal what we need to know at the proper time in order to keep moving forward.

My desire had been to preach that Sunday morning, but God had a different plan, and all I could do was to submit to this part of His will. Ian's text was from 2 Samuel 24:24. It was a sermon that only another pastor could deliver to a congregation that was standing at the crossroads of obedience. It was at that very moment that God pulled back a portion of the veil that had been covering His will for First Baptist Atlanta. None of us, at this point, knew what God knew concerning the future He had planned for this faithful congregation and the ministry of In Touch. He could see perfectly the steps that were in front of us, but we could not. This was step one in an entire staircase of steps that continue on today.

Second Samuel 24:24 records a conversation between King David and the owner of a piece of land that David wanted to purchase as a place of sacrifice and rededication to the Lord. He had made a costly mistake by counting the fighting men in Israel's army. It was a human desire that tempted him to do something that was not in keeping with his life of faith before the Lord. God punished David and Israel severely for this mistake. When David realized that God had stopped His angel outside the city of Jerusalem, he rushed out to meet the Lord.

David was a man after God's own heart, not because he was talented or smart, but because he loved the Lord. Deep inside of him was a desire to obey and please God. Usually, before there is a great outpouring of God's blessing through answered prayer, there is a season of repentance and personal cleansing. Ian's sermon prepared the hearts of the people for a mighty miracle—one that did not stop for months to come. As he closed the services that day, Ian asked the people in his best Australian voice, "Have you given to the Lord that which cost you something?" A silence fell over the sanctuary, and then the altar filled with people who realized God was calling them to give sacrificially to His work in the church and through His ministry of In Touch.

The following week, I was back in the pulpit preaching and wondering what God was going to do. At the close of the service, people began to come forward bringing their sacrificial offerings to the Lord. It goes without saying that God provided the money we needed to purchase the cameras debt free. My heart was overwhelmed with gratitude to the Lord for His faithfulness and for a brief moment thought, "Well, that is that. We have the cameras and now we are set." Little did I know, but God was already at work on an even bigger set of challenges that would stretch our faith beyond anything we could imagine.

There may be seasons when you feel as though you are not really doing that much. You may even wonder if you are moving toward the goal He has given you. You are, however, and the exciting part of living within His will is that you will never grow bored. Even when you do not see His hand working, He is moving and positioning you for His purpose and to fulfill His future plan.

My challenge to you is found in 2 Samuel 24:24. In order to know God's will you have to commit yourself to Him. Have you given Him just what you feel is convenient or have you given Him something—every area of your life—that costs you something. The man who owned the field where David was going to offer his sacrifice to the Lord wanted to just give it to the king. However, David refused because he knew that the sacrifice he offered to God needed to be one of obedience—it had to cost him something.

## *A Prayer that Changes Lives*

Many people try to find the will of God for their lives. They discuss it with friends, pray about it, and read countless books on the subject without discovering what God has for them. The reason many miss it is because they are too caught up in the details of life to turn their faces toward heaven with open hearts and say, "Here am I, [Lord]. Send me!" (Isaiah 6:8).

In his letter to the Colossian church, Paul writes his prayer for the believers in that fellowship. It was a prayer for their personal spiritual growth so they could fulfill God's will. "For this reason also, since the day we heard of it, we have not ceased to pray for you and to ask that you may be filled with the knowledge of His will in all spiritual wisdom and understanding, so that you will walk in a manner worthy of the Lord, to please Him in all respects, bearing fruit in every good work and increasing in the knowledge of God" (Colossians 1:9-10).

Paul doesn't stop with the words written above. He continues because there is more for us to consider when it comes to the will of God: "Strengthened with all power, according to [God's] glorious might, for the attaining of all steadfastness and patience; joyously giving thanks to the Father, who has qualified us to share in the inheritance of the saints in Light" (vv. 11-12).

*When we are walking in the light of God's will, our lives will take on the characteristics that are like Him (Colossians 2:3; 2 Corinthians 4:11, 13).* We will have a sense of strength that is not derived from human ability but from a heart totally devoted to Christ. God's will involves His purpose, plan, and desire for each one of us individually. Therefore,

when we come to discover His will, we can ask Him
three questions:

- *Lord, what is Your will for my life or this
  particular situation?*
- *How can I discover it?*
- *What is Your desire for me—what would
  please You?*

There will be times when God will answer these
questions, and we will know what He wants us to
do in a given set of circumstances. However, many
times, we must spend time seeking His will and
plan. We knew that God wanted the In Touch
broadcast on television, but we could not conceive
His greater plan for the future. Many times, He
only gives us the sight we need in order to do what
He wants us to do next. I doubt if anyone on our
staff could have handled God revealing all that was
going to come our way over the next ten, twenty,
or thirty years. God's plan was too awesome. We
would have been overwhelmed by it. Many times,
this is the very reason He does not reveal all that is
involved in His plan. *However, we can know His will
for us today if we surrender our lives to Him.*

Those who do not do this will miss God's plan

for their lives. There is no other way to put it. Either we live submitted and committed lives, or we miss the opportunity to experience His blessings and end up losing what could have been a great victory.

## *God's Challenge to Us*

I have had people tell me, "I just don't believe in all of this." They go and do whatever they want to do and end up in a miserable state because God has told us that we were created for Him and not for ourselves (Colossians 1:16). This means that He has a plan, and His desire is for us to live it out. When we get off track, life becomes very rocky and rough. The prodigal son believed he had a better plan than the one his father had for him. So, he packed up his gear and walked away. This is what happened in the Garden of Eden. Satan tempted Adam and Eve to question God's plan. "For God knows that in the day you eat from it your eyes will be opened, and you will be like God, knowing good and evil" (Genesis 3:5).

Eve realized there was a plan in place, but now she had to make a decision to either stick with the course that God had given them or take a different path. She chose the different path and rebelled against God by sinning and disobeying Him. What heartache she must have felt after taking a bite of the forbidden fruit! There is no way to disobey God and not realize that you have made a huge mistake. The damage was done, but God did not reject His creation. He knew their response to the enemy would lead to sin and mankind's fall.

He also knows what our response will be at every turn in this life. He desires the best for us. In fact, His will and plan is one of hope and blessing (Jeremiah 29:11). However, we must choose to obey, and then we will receive the blessing. God's desired will for us is that we will walk according to His plan for our lives.

## *A Promise and a Plan*

Someone reading this book may think, "I have messed up, and this is the first time I have heard any of this." Let me remind you again that God still has a will for your life. No matter how badly you have messed up, He takes the broken pieces of your life, and through the power of His unconditional love and the blood of His Son, Jesus Christ, He put the pieces back together. Then He says to you, "From this point on, you are walking within my circumstantial will for your life. In light of all that is behind you, I am going to take you from where you are now to a place of blessing. As you place your trust in Me as Your Savior, I will show you how to live out the rest of your life; with My help and strength, you will live as an overcomer and not as a person who has been defeated."

The apostle Paul prayed that we would be made strong so we could fulfill God's purpose. He also prayed that we would have the spiritual wisdom we need to avoid making costly mistakes that jeopardize our walk of faith with Jesus Christ. However, when we do, God has a plan in place for our restoration so that we can begin to live in the center of His will. You don't have to flip a coin or guess what His will for your life is. You can know.

I think of the many young people, who head off to college each year, hoping that they are making the right decision and career choice. *When we think of God's will for our lives, we need to realize that He assumes full responsibility for telling us what it is. It is our responsibility to discover it (Matthew 7:8).*

No general goes to war without a battle plan, and God does not expect us to go through life without one either.

It is the nature of God to reveal His will to us. Second, it is the promise of God to show us what His plan is for our lives. In Psalm 32, God promises to reveal His will to us, "I will instruct you and teach you in the way which you should go; I will counsel you with My eye upon you" (v. 8). This promise is followed by a word of caution: "Do not be as the horse or as the mule which have no understanding, whose trappings include bit and bridle to hold them in check" (v. 9). This Scripture is mirrored by the words of Proverbs 3:5-7, "Trust in the Lord with all your heart and do not lean on your own understanding. In all your ways acknowledge Him, and He will make your paths straight. Do not be wise in your own eyes; fear the Lord and turn away from evil."

## *His Promise Leads to Spiritual Victory*

God wants to make His promise and plan for your life very clear. It is part of His character to clarify what He desires for us to do. There will be times when He will map out the plan we are to follow. Other times, He will ask us to walk forward by faith trusting Him to provide all we need when we need it. In Psalm 16, David writes, "You will make known to me the path of life; in your presence is fullness of joy; in Your right hand there are pleasures forever" (v.11).

I want to address a subject that I mentioned earlier, and that is the importance of the Word of God in your life. God speaks to us primarily through His Word. He also speaks to us through the presence of the Holy Spirit and words spoken by a godly friend or pastor. At no time will the counsel of the Spirit go against what is written in God's Word, and neither should the counsel we receive from others. What we hear and read always should line up with God's Word. This is because His Word is our life's compass. In it, we find direction for the decisions we need to make today and in the future.

If you want to find God's will for your life, you have to begin by reading and studying His Word. This is where He will begin to reveal His plan, and it is where we start to understand the nature of God. You can't know Him apart from His Word.

Yet, many people try to do this very thing. They go to church on Sundays hoping they will find an answer to their problems. They turn on the television praying that someone will provide a solution to their situation. Many preachers, today, will tell their audiences that they can experience a "break through" in what they are facing, but apart from the Word of God, this is impossible.

The way we come to know God is by reading the Bible. How we learn to live life within the framework of His will is by studying and applying the principles given to us within scripture. Once a person understands this truth, he or she can know God's will for most situations.

In 1 Samuel 23:2, David learned to seek God's wisdom before heading off to battle. A group of men came to him saying, "'Behold, the Philistines are fighting against Keilah and are plundering the threshing floors.' So David inquired of the Lord, saying, 'Shall I go and attack these Philistines?' And the Lord said to David, 'Go and attack the Philistines and deliver Keilah.'" God gave him the wisdom he needed, but he had to ask the Lord for guidance, and we do, too.

## *A New Way of Living*

He may not tell you whether to wear brown or
black shoes tomorrow, but you can know whether
He wants you to move forward or stay where you
are. His Word will help you to learn how He thinks;
and once you begin to understand this, you will be
able to begin to know His plan for your life.

It is not just the study of God's Word that will
help you in your discovery of His plan for your life;
it is the understanding that, once you accept Christ
as your Savior, you become a new person. Life
changes dramatically. You are no longer operating
under the old system. A new one is in operation.
Paul writes in 2 Corinthians, "Therefore if anyone is
in Christ, he is a new creature; the old things passed
away; behold new things have come," (5:17).

God also reveals His will to us through circumstances. Even though he was in prison, Paul wrote
to the Philippian church saying, "I want you to
know, brethren that my circumstances have turned
out for the greater progress of the gospel, so that
my imprisonment in the cause of Christ has become
well known throughout the whole praetorian guard
and to everyone else" (Philippians 1:12-13). Even

though Paul's circumstances did not look good,
God used them to accomplish His will. We must be
willing to go the extra mile with God. Just as we
said earlier when talking about Abraham, God
instructed him to move forward and he obeyed
based of the fact that the One who was speaking to
him was a sovereign God.

Your circumstances may be very trying, and you
do not understand how God will ever gain glory
from what you are facing. He will, and if you set
the focus of your heart on knowing and pleasing
Him, not only will you experience His blessings,
but those around you will be blessed as well. *Jesus
has promised never to leave you.* This means every
single moment of your life, He is living within you
(John 15:4,7).

# CHAPTER TEN

# The Adventure Begins

The weather report was shocking. For the fourth time in a year, a hurricane was heading for the Gulf of Mexico and for Florida. Despite the prayers of millions of Christians, this storm, like the ones before it, seemed determined to bring destruction to a massive area of land that had not recovered from the earlier storms. There was a state of panic as people either evacuated or remained glued to their television screens watching news and weather reports.

Somewhere in the hurricane's path was a Christian retirement community that also housed an assisted living and nursing home facility. As news media broadcast live reports concerning the storm's path and the people at the national weather station tracked its every move, the residents of this small Florida community did what they had practiced many times; they calmly walked to their designated storm shelter—a parking garage that had been out-

fitted with removable storm siding—and settled in
for what promised to be a very long night. They
had been instructed to bring lounge chairs, water,
and snacks.

## *Faith in an All-Powerful God*

As the evening approached, residents became aware
that they could receive a direct hit from the hurricane. However, instead of striking fear in their
hearts, the howling wind and the turbulent rains
only created what one resident called "a cozy envi-
ronment." Finally, someone began to sing an old
hymn, and soon others joined. Words of prayer and
praise also filled the dusty parking deck, and it
became a shelter of peace for God's people in a time
of horrendous trial.

Hours later, the danger had passed and residents
were allowed to return to their homes. Many joined
hands and formed a human chain as they walked
back to their homes and to their rooms. Suddenly, a
glorious sunset broke through the clouds and the
residents looked up to see the sky streaked with
color. Even in this time of trial, it was as if the peace
of God hovered over them.

How many of us would dare to look at our broken circumstances and storm-driven lives and see the color of a sunset or a sunrise? God does every time, and He tells us,

*I know the plans I have for you (Jeremiah 29:11).*
*I have inscribed your name on the palms of*
*    My hand (Isaiah 49:16).*
*Nothing can separate you from My love*
*    (Romans 8:35).*
*My love casts out fear (1 John 4:18).*
*I will never leave you (John 14:18).*
*My thoughts of you are too numerous to count*
*    (Psalm 40:5).*
*I go to prepare a place for you and you will be*
*    with Me (John 14:2).*

We are never outside God's overarching plan. It may seem that we have taken a wrong turn, gotten off track, or that the sorrows of this life have caught up with us; but God is never surprised by our circumstances, and He is never out of control. There are no storms too great and no problems too deep for Him to solve. No matter what you may face, when you surrender your life and your situation to

Him, God will place a sense of peace deep within your heart, and you will come to know Him in a more intimate way.

## *His Plan Never Changes*

*The situations of life may change, but God never does (Hebrew 13:8).* He does not alter His determined plan for our lives. We can step away from it, but He still has a determined will that is at work molding and shaping us and leading us back to Him.

Many people make mistakes and worry that they have disappointed God, but we cannot disappoint an all-knowing God. He knew how we would respond even before temptation pulled at our hearts. He is committed to loving us through the sorrow of our sin and helping us get back on track.

Someone reading these words cannot believe life can be lived without the influence of drugs or alcohol, but it can. Others wonder how God can possibly have a plan for their lives now that their spouse has left them, but He does. He is not distracted or changed by our circumstances. He is our deliverer and His truth will set us free from the bondage of sin, doubt, fear, worry, and anxiety. It heals our wounded hearts and opens up our lives to the possibility of being used once again, or maybe for the first time, for God's glory.

Paul writes to the believers living in the city of Colossae, "For this reason also, since the day we heard of it, we have not ceased to pray for you and to ask that you may be filled with the knowledge of His will in all spiritual wisdom and understanding" (Colossians 1:9). Once we realize that God has a promise for our lives, we begin to understand that this promise involves every area of life. *It doesn't matter whether we are young or old; God's plan begins before we take our first breath and does not end until we are standing in His presence.*

"God causes all things to work together for good to those who love [Him], to those who are called according to His purpose" (Romans 8:28). This is God's promised will to every man and woman who comes to know Him as Savior and Lord. No one is excluded from His plan or purpose. However, we are the ones who must take hold of this promise and choose to live our lives for Him.

Peter could have remained on shore the day that Jesus asked to use his fishing boat. He could have

said, "No way! I am not going to launch my boat
and go back out on the sea. I just got back from
being out there and, to be honest, there's no fish.
Today is not a good day to go fishing." However, we
know that Peter did not say any of this. He looked
into the eyes of Jesus and saw something much deeper than he had ever seen. Within the eyes of Christ
was all that he had prayed to know and discover.
Though he did not know how to express it, Peter
knew a new world of hope and possibility awaited
him, and the first step to experiencing this was
summed up in his words of obedience, "Master . . .
because of your instruction I will let down the nets"
(Luke 5:5).

A few minutes later, Peter's nets began to fill
with fish. The catch was so great that they began
to break, and he called to his friends to come and
help him. They responded by sailing their boats to
the same spot. However, these boats also filled up
and began to sink. Peter "fell down at Jesus' feet,
saying, 'Go away from me Lord, for I am a sinful
man'" (Luke 5:8). None of this was a result of
luck or coincidence. There is no such thing in the
life of a believer. This was a planned event—a

moment in Peter's life that fit perfectly with the will of God.

## *An Exciting Adventure Begins*

Bending over to touch the shoulder of His new disciple, Jesus said, "Do not fear, from now on you will be catching men" (v. 10). When Peter and the others reached the shore, they left everything and followed Christ. Their greatest desire had come true. They had found the Savior and they were right on course to begin an amazing journey that would last for eternity.

*God wants you to know that He has a wondrous promise for your life. It is a promise that involves His perfect plan and one that will bring joy, hope, and countless opportunities.* Will you raise your sails, head out into deep water, and allow the winds of His purpose and victory to blow through your life so others will come to know the Savior's love, too?

# Have You Accepted God's Greatest Gift

Our heavenly Father has prepared many special gifts and blessings for His children. However, the greatest gift is the gift of eternal life that He gives to those who come to Him through faith in His Son Jesus. If you have never invited Him to be your Savior and Lord, you can right now by praying this simple prayer:

*Father, I know that I am a sinner. I believe Jesus died on the cross for my sins and paid my sin debt in full cleansing me of my past failures and guilt. I surrender control of my life to You today. Make me the person You have designed me to be. I pray this in Jesus' name. Amen.*

If you sincerely prayed this prayer to God, then according to God's Word, you have been born again! (Scripture) I want to challenge you to take positive steps to grow in your new faith. Please

take time to visit www.charlesstanleyinstitute.com
and become involved in our study program. Also,
be sure to tell someone of your decision to follow
Jesus and find a church that will teach the uncom-
promised truth of God's Word. Today is the first
day of a journey that will someday lead you into
the presence of your heavenly Father, who has
loved you since the beginning of time.